SO-BHR-384

Traditional Bowhunting for Whitetails

0 11557 03308 3

Traditional Bowhunting for Whitetails

Brian Sorrells

STACKPOLE BOOKS

Copyright © 2006 by Stackpole Books

Published by
STACKPOLE BOOKS
5067 Ritter Road
Mechanicsburg, PA 17055
www.stackpolebooks.com

Printed in the United States

First edition

Cover photo by the author
Cover design by Caroline Stover

10 9 8 7 6 5 4 3 2 1

Library of Congress Cataloging-in-Publication Data
Sorrells, Brian J.
  Traditional bowhunting for whitetails / Brian Sorrells.
    p. cm.
  Includes index.
  ISBN-13: 978-0-8117-3308-3 (alk. paper)
  ISBN-10: 0-8117-3308-4 (alk. paper)
  1. White-tailed deer hunting. 2. Bowhunting. I. Title.

SK301.S692 2006
799.2'7652—dc22
                                                        2006003656

Contents

Foreword

Traditional bowhunting, like many outdoor activities, carries its own risks. It is your responsibility to make sure that your bow and arrows are in good working order. In addition, the responsible hunter always wears a fall-restraint device when hunting from a treestand. Obey all applicable federal, state, and local hunting rules and regulations regarding equipment, seasons, and bag limits, and never hunt on private property without expressed consent from the property owner. Finally, always make sure you are in adequate physical condition to participate in an activity that will require physical exertion.

The author and publisher of this book should not be held responsible for any damage or injury incurred by or to another party as a result of any of the facts, ideas, opinions, or advice contained in this book.

Acknowledgments

When undertaking such a major endeavor as writing a book, the writer knows that seldom does it get finished without help and support from others. This project was no different for me. There are people who deserve a tip of the hat (and sometimes much more) for their patience and assistance, and I aim to see that they get it.

First, I would like to thank and recognize my dad, Bill Sorrells (August 17, 1925, to October 1, 2000) for teaching me to love hunting, fishing, and the outdoors. I miss you every day, Dad.

My appreciation also goes to my mom for her support, and to Lowell and Eldean Moffitt, my aunt and uncle, who allowed Dad and I to spend so much time together hunting on their beautiful farm.

Thanks to Charlie Bliss, who introduced me to the world of traditional archery and who taught me that change is only good if it's for the better.

Thank you to Jane Chastain, a wonderful doctor of veterinary medicine, who allows me to hunt on her farm and, even though she has dedicated her life to helping animals, understands that hunting is a necessary part of many people's lives.

Thanks to my beautiful wife, Jamie, and my wonderful children, Brandi, Jailin, Rachel, Marty, and Claire. All of you are an inspiration to me. Thanks for your patience.

Thank you to Jay Strangis at *Peterson's Bowhunting Magazine* for allowing me the opportunity to write a column now and then.

A special thank you to Dale Karch and Dean Vanderhorst at 3 Rivers Archery for loaning me the Tomahawk Thunderstorm takedown longbow featured in several photographs in this book.

Finally, thanks to Don Thomas at *Traditional Bowhunter Magazine* for all of his support and advice over time. "Thanks" falls far too short to describe my gratitude.

And, to all of you reading this, thank you and God bless you.

Introduction

Over the years, I've done a lot of hunting with traditional bows, from small game like rabbits and squirrels, to predators such as the wary coyote, to hunting caribou with the Innuit Indians south of the Arctic Circle. Of all the animals I've chased, none thrills my heart as much as the white-tailed deer. I guess that's because even though the animal can be found in just about every little woodlot across the United States, its very nature makes it a tremendous challenge. It's no surprise that white-tailed deer are the number-one game animal pursued across the country, both by traditionalists with bows and those who hunt with rifles, shotguns, compounds, and crossbows.

Of those of us who pursue the whitetail, traditional bowhunters are a special group. For us, it's the chase, rather than the kill, that provides the most satisfaction, and it's the journey, not the destination, that gives us memories of close encounters with big bucks on warm autumn afternoons or under stark winter skies.

The bows we carry are as much a part of the tradition as deer hunting itself. Though materials and workmanship have improved over the years, the basic shape and simplicity of our bows have not.

The very nature of the bow dictates that we *must* be close to our quarry before we take a shot. Actually seeing a deer's eyelashes and hearing the animal breathe are what makes the hunt so thrilling, and often feeling that nearness is as good as taking him or her home with you. To the bowhunter, the hunt becomes a lot more personal. Because our weapon gives us no advantage over the deer we're hunting, we feel a greater connection to the animals and their environment than those who choose to hunt with more modern equipment. Traditional bowhunters are true stewards of our natural resources. For that reason and others, this book's focus will not be on how to hunt trophy white-tailed bucks. Enough books already cover that subject. And, if you read far enough, you'll learn of my true feelings about trophies in general.

White-tailed deer and traditional bows are a perfect match. A marriage made in heaven. In this book, I try to bring that connection together by sharing what has worked for me time and again and by providing a little food for thought along with a few stories. In the process, I hope that you, the reader, develop or renew your passion for the pursuit of the white-tailed deer with traditional tackle.

Hunting itself in recent years has come under fire from various organizations, such as the Humane Society of the United States and People for the Ethical Treatment of Animals. As true bowhunters, we must do everything within our power to preserve our heritage and protect it from those who would like to take away our rights and privileges to pursue game in any form. To me, traditional bowhunting is the purest form of pursuit. Therefore, the traditional bowhunter has the greatest responsibility to uphold game laws and display morality, ethics, and sportsmanship above and beyond what is expected of hunters in general. We are the gentlemen and women of bowhunting. We refuse to accept technology as a "crutch," and even when everyone around us is running to catch up with the latest models of sights or rangefinders, we continue to do things the old-fashioned way. By accepting the limitations of the traditional bow, we become better hunters, and better people in the process.

The next time you head for the whitetail woods, stop and remember this: It's not a head on the wall or the meat in the freezer that makes a whitetail hunter successful. It's continuing the tradition of those who went before us, hunters such as Fred Bear and Howard Hill, and teaching the traditions of morals, ethics, and the challenge of the traditional bow to those who come after us. Only then will the heritage of white-tailed deer hunting with traditional archery tackle continue for generations to come.

- 1 -

Traditional Tackle for White-tailed Deer

One of the great things about hunting whitetails with traditional tackle is the fact that you don't need a bow with a lot of draw weight to take a deer cleanly and quickly. Accuracy and a sharp broadhead are much more important than arrow speed. Because whitetails are relatively thin-skinned—the shoulder blade is the worst obstacle a traditional bowhunter has to worry about—and so plentiful, white-tailed deer hunting is available to people who, for various reasons, can't hunt bigger game or travel a long way from home to hunt. In this chapter, we'll talk about what you need to be a successful whitetail hunter with traditional archery tackle.

The ultimate goal of the stickbow hunter is the accurate placement of a razor-sharp broadhead. An arrow that passes through either the heart or BOTH lungs will cause any animal to go down in the matter of a few minutes, if not quicker. A deer hunter using traditional equipment should never have to struggle to come to full draw, and he or she should be able to do it repeatedly without tiring.

For many years, we thought that the draw weight for a traditional hunting bow had to be at least 60 pounds, and preferably 70 or 75, before the arrow would achieve enough speed to lethally penetrate anything but the smallest game. Although that may have been true years ago, the efficiency of today's bow designs and the materials used to build them allow the traditional bowhunter to be conservative in draw weight and still get excellent performance. In fact, modern stickbows can shoot as fast as some of the older round-wheeled compounds of the same draw weight. So, we can throw all of the preconceived notions and old wives' tales out the window and start from scratch by building the ideal traditional setup for whitetails.

THE IDEAL TRADITIONAL BOW

Traditional bows are extremely accurate as long as the archer controls the bow and not vice versa. Draw weight is important not only from the standpoint of how well the archer can draw, anchor, and release the bowstring, but also by the minimum draw weight required by your particular state. In my home state of Indiana and in many other states, the minimum draw weight for **any** bow is 35 pounds. Most traditional archers should be able to draw and anchor a 35-pound stickbow with little problem.

The archer should be able to point the bow at a specific target, draw the bowstring **straight** back without pointing the bow up or down, and anchor for six to eight seconds without shaking. If you can't do that with your bow, then you need to either get a lighter draw weight bow or undertake a strength training regimen to build up the shoulder and back muscles you use to shoot a traditional bow. The Bowfit strength trainer can help you do just that. It consists of a handle and a series of large rubber bands that reproduce the action of drawing a traditional bow. If you don't have the money or desire to invest in the Bowfit unit, you can always use your bow to accomplish the same result. Simply take your bow to full draw and hold at anchor as long as you can. Let down slowly, rest a few seconds, and repeat. Do this with both arms to ensure

Every traditional bowhunter should be able to draw his bow straight back to anchor.

There is a length and style of bow to fit every traditional bowhunter.
Left to right: 68-inch Martin longbow, 64-inch Indian recurve, 62-inch
3 River's Archery Tomahawk longbow, and 52-inch Bear recurve.

that your back muscles get equal training and you maintain the same balance of strength on both sides. If you perform this exercise three to four times a week, you soon will see how your increased strength will allow you to draw more easily and hold at full draw longer. By using a bow that you can control rather than struggling with every shot, you will discover greater accuracy in your hunting.

Depending on your physical characteristics and the type of hunting you do the most, bow style and length also come into play. For instance, a taller bowhunter with a longer than normal draw length will enjoy more comfort and better shooting with a traditional bow of a longer overall length, which produces less finger pinch and less of a string angle at full draw. A taller bowhunter also has more "ground clearance" and has to worry less about the lower limb tip striking the ground or the platform of a treestand during a shot. On the other hand, shorter bowhunters generally have shorter draw lengths and do well with shorter bows.

As for bow styles, both longbows and recurves are available in nearly the same lengths nowadays. Years ago, before modern design and materials came into play, the shorter hunting recurve provided smoother motion and better shooting than the longer longbow. But today, modern longbows are available in shorter overall lengths and produce arrow speeds and kinetic energy equivalent to their recurve cousins with none of the hand shock found in the old designs.

Due to the growing popularity of traditional archery, high-quality traditional bows are now being made by many well-known compound bow manufacturers. PSE, Martin Archery, and the Fred Bear Bowhunting Equipment Company all make very high-quality longbows and recurves at reasonable prices. Even Matthews Solo-Cam produces some really good-looking longbows and recurves. The archer looking for custom-made traditional bows can find them from such skilled artisans as Ron and Debbie King at Fox Archery in Wallowa, Oregon, the "Widow Workers" at Black Widow Cus-

Custom bows come with personal touches such as your name on the bow.

tom Bows in Nixa, Missouri, and Keith Chastain of Wapiti Long-bows and Recurves in Lakewood, Colorado, to name a few.

Although custom bows cost more than "mass-produced" stick-bows built by such companies as Martin Archery or Fred Bear, the added cost often is worth the quality and workmanship and usually includes some nice extras, ranging from placing your name on the bow to installing custom-shaped grips with special inlays, exotic woods for riser and limbs, and antler limb tip laminations. I've owned many custom bows over the years, including three I currently use that are among the best I've found so far: a 62-inch takedown longbow from Black Widow, a 60-inch bamboo longbow from Keith Chastain of Wapiti Archery, and a 60-inch yew longbow from Fox Archery. Even in shorter lengths, these wonderful little bows sacrifice nothing in speed and smoothness.

If you travel with your bows a great deal, a takedown longbow or recurve might be worth the investment and save valuable space in your vehicle or on the airplane. Takedown recurve bows are

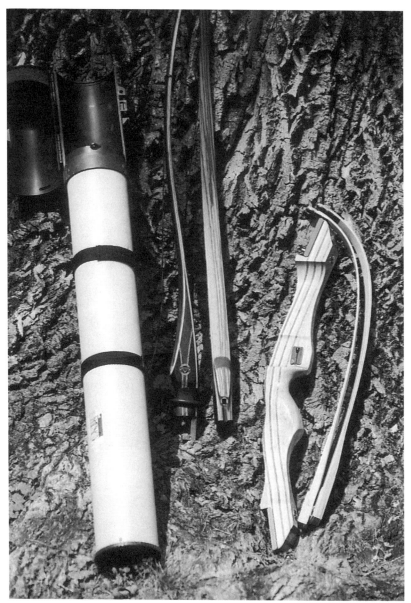

Takedown bows, such as the Tomahawk Thunderstorm longbow on the left and the Indian recurve on the right, fit in a small case and make great travel bows. Note the "T-hawk" takedown system on the longbow. Once you roll down the rubber sleeve, it looks like a one-piece bow.

available from both custom bowyers and bigger companies such as Martin Archery and Bear. Two- and three-piece longbows are generally only available from custom bowmakers. With a takedown bow, you get the convenience of easy transportation without sacrificing any performance. All of the takedown longbows and recurves that I've owned shoot the same as their one-piece counterparts.

The decision to shoot a longbow, a recurve bow, a flatbow, or a selfbow rests on you. Each style has its own diehard following, but how it kills deer depends on whether the archer behind the bow is proficient and up to the task. To be successful with your chosen tackle, you have to be honest with yourself. If you already own a bow that fits you, is easily handled and is in serviceable condition, then you're all set. But if your bow is an old hand-me-down with problems or if you're trying to fit the bow rather than the bow fitting you, then think seriously about investing in a bow that you know will last and fit you and your shooting style. I've seen too many good traditional bowhunters try to hunt with ill-fitting bows that either belonged to a relative or they picked up cheap at a pawn shop. Do yourself a favor and make sure you have a good bow that you enjoy shooting and that you can shoot well.

With modern recurves and longbows performing better and lasting longer than their predecessors, today's stickbow hunters have it better than ever before. Failures such as delamination of bow limbs or failed glue lines are few and far between, thanks to modern high-strength epoxies and advances in design and technology. With proper routine care, your traditional bow should last you for many years. To maintain your bow, use the checklist below as a guideline before every hunt and shooting session.

BOW MAINTENANCE CHECKLIST

1. Check the bow for cracks in glue lines or nicks that may affect the integrity of the bow. Minor scratches and nicks in the finish should be repaired with superglue to keep out

moisture. Never shoot a bow with cracked or twisted limbs or any major damage to the handle or riser. Make sure any insert bushings in the handle or riser are clean and secure with no radiating cracks.

2. On takedown bows, make sure all hardware is tight and in good working order. Lubrication is usually not required, but bowstring wax does a good job of preventing rust on metal parts. Check for limb alignment before stringing the bow.

3. Wax the bowstring regularly and make sure it is free from broken strands. Regardless of whether your bowstring is Dacron or one of the newer materials, a broken strand can spell disaster for your favorite bow and yourself, if the string should break while you're holding or shooting the bow.

4. Make sure the shelf rest and strike plate are firmly attached and not worn out.

5. Check to ensure that any bow quiver you use is tight and in good repair.

ARROWS, THE REAL KEY TO SUCCESS

Regardless of what bow style you shoot, the arrow is the piece of equipment that really makes the difference. Without a correctly spined arrow, even the most expensive traditional bow is useless. An arrow of the right length and spine will stabilize more quickly when it leaves the bow and will fly straight to the target, allowing all of the arrow's energy to travel in a straight line rather than being wasted in oscillation.

Arrow weight also figures heavily into downrange perform-ance. Bowhunters have debated arrow weight versus arrow speed for many years. Compound bow shooters believe that the faster an arrow flies, the better it performs. With their average arrow approaching speeds of 300 feet per second, they can afford to think that way. Stickbow shooters, on the other hand, know that 180 feet per second is the average speed of their arrows, and anything over 200 feet per second is scorching. Therefore, our concern is a healthy balance of arrow speed *and* arrow weight.

A traditional bow works most efficiently when we shoot an arrow somewhere around 9 to 11 grains of arrow weight per pound of bow weight. In other words, if our draw weight is 50 pounds, our finished hunting arrow should weigh somewhere between 450 and 510 grains. A heavy arrow does two things at once. First, it absorbs more of the energy stored in the bow's limbs, allowing the arrow to carry more kinetic energy to the target. Second, by absorbing more of the bow's energy, it makes for a much quieter shooting bow. When you shoot a light arrow, its lower mass prevents it from absorbing as much kinetic energy and this energy remains in the bow, heard as noise and felt as hand shock. A heavier arrow may not get to the deer as quickly as a lighter arrow, but the deer is not likely to jump the string because of bow noise. The heavier arrow also will penetrate deeper because it carries more of the bow's energy with it.

The deer hunting stickbow enthusiast has three types of arrows available. Wood, the oldest and arguably the most traditional of all arrow shaft materials, can be found in spine weights to match any hunting weight bow. Aluminum, straight and true, makes a fantastic hunting arrow and is more durable than wood. Carbon, the newest material on the market, is as straight as aluminum and the toughest, most durable arrow shaft material.

Since each type of material has the ability to be tuned to fly correctly, I recommend shooting whichever shaft makes you happiest. Keep in mind that each shaft material has its own eccentricities. Wood, the hardest to work with, has a tendency to "wander" and requires occasional straightening even after it's sealed and fletched. Wood shafts also vary the most in weight and spine, resulting in slightly different characteristics between shafts from the same bunch. Wood shafts must be tapered at each end to accept nocks

Aluminum (two left arrows), carbon (two center arrows), and wood (two right arrows) all shoot from traditional bows when tuned properly. The raw wood shaft on the right is tapered to accept a nock and point. WOOD ARROWS *COURTESY OF 3 RIVERS ARCHERY*

and field points or broadheads. When the time comes to refletch a wood shaft, great care must be taken not to remove wood with the old feathers. Wood arrows vary in price, from relatively inexpensive bundles of raw shafts to very expensive custom-made arrows. All in all, they require a lot of work, but some traditional bowhunters wouldn't use anything else.

Aluminum is probably the easiest shaft to work with, as it can be cut to length with a hack saw or even a pipe-cutting tool. It's weatherproof, requires no hand straightening, and is easy to refletch. The downside is that aluminum doesn't stand up that well to abuse, especially after a glancing blow or a head-on shot into something very hard. Aluminum shafts are relatively inexpensive, even if you order them premade as finished arrows. They are available in several different anodized finishes from plain brown to a finish that looks strikingly like a footed cedar arrow. They even come in camouflage patterns to match your hunting attire.

Carbon, the most modern arrow shaft material, receives the least respect from purist bowhunters who claim that it is not "traditional" enough to shoot from a stickbow. Personally, I think that if a bowhunter allows carbon and fiberglass laminations in his or her hunting bow, then what's wrong with shooting carbon arrows? I use them myself. They do have certain requirements that make them harder to work with than aluminum, but the benefits are more than worth the added effort. For instance, carbon shafts must be cut with a high-speed shaft cutter using an abrasive blade to assure a clean cut with no broken carbon fibers. Also, when the fletching needs to be replaced, great care must be taken not to remove any of the carbon shaft material with the old feathers, something that can be avoided simply by using a vinyl cresting wrap. Cresting wraps come in many colors and patterns and allow for very distinctive arrows with none of the mess and trouble normally associated with cresting paints. When the time comes to refletch the arrow, simply dunk the fletched end of the arrow into a

Vinyl cresting wraps work on any shaft material and make a beautiful hunting arrow.

pot of boiling water and remove both the wrap and old feathers at one time. Apply another wrap and you're ready to refletch.

Carbon arrows are by far the most durable arrows on the market. I shoot the Grizzlystik carbon shaft from Alaska Bowhunting Supply, and these shafts have been shot through sheet metal, into railroad ties, and even into solid rock, all with no damage other than a few scratches in the finish. Although made of the most expensive shaft material on the market, carbon arrows won't have to be replaced unless you manage to damage one (not likely) or lose one.

While we're on the subject of fletching and cresting wraps, let's discuss color. I like bright fletching and cresting wraps on my arrows because they help me to see them. Deer don't see colors, at least not as we see them, so bright colors will not alert deer to our presence. Arrows with dark or muted fletching are difficult to follow in flight, making it even harder to see where your arrow hits the deer, something you have to know to decide when and how to take up the blood trail. Bright cresting or fletching not only makes the arrow easier to spot in flight and against the hide of a deer, but it makes the arrow easier to find, especially when we miss.

When shooting a deer, even with a bow with a light draw weight, it's quite possible to shoot an arrow completely through the animal. The key is to make sure that your bow is set up properly and that your arrow is correctly tuned to your particular bow and tipped with a sharp broadhead. To achieve optimum arrow flight, you must have the correct combination of arrow spine, arrow length, and point weight. A correctly spined arrow will flex around the riser when the bowstring is released and straighten out quickly with little oscillation soon after it leaves the bow. Arrow spine is determined by the length of the shaft, the diameter of the shaft, and the thickness of the shaft walls, but it is influenced by the weight of the field point or broadhead on the end of the shaft. The best way to optimize your arrow flight is with a method called bare shaft tuning. The archer begins with a shaft about 4 inches longer than needed and gradually shortens the shaft until the arrow flies fairly straight and hits squarely into a soft bag target, all with no feather guidance. For those of you who don't know how it works, let me briefly explain.

Start out with the arrow shaft of your choice, of the correct spine for your draw length and bow weight as indicated on the spine chart for that particular shaft. If using wood arrows, you may want to get several different spine weights to be on the safe side. This shaft should be about 4 inches longer than your minimum arrow length. The minimum arrow length is your draw length plus $1^1/2$ inches. Mark this measurement on your bare shaft with a permanent marker before you begin bare shaft tuning. The shaft should be without feathers and have only a nock and a field point equal to the weight of your favorite broadhead. This is crucial because once your bare shaft tuning has been completed, any change in point weight will affect arrow flight. Check to make sure the brace height on your bow is within the range recommended by the manufacturer, and place a nocking point on the bowstring about $1/2$ inch above the arrow shelf. Make sure that any accessories you plan to have on the bow when you're hunting, such as string silencers and bow quivers (loaded to capacity with arrows), are in place before you begin the process. The reason we start with the nocking point so high will become clear a little later.

Stand about 30 feet from the target, and shoot an arrow at the center of it. One of three things will happen. Keep in mind that because we've started with the nocking point too high on the bowstring, the nock on the end of the arrow will be higher than the spot where the field point sticks in the target. We're looking to see whether the nock end of the arrow is oriented to where the point of the arrow is sticking in to the target in the left and right plane. If the nock is to the right, then the arrow has too much spine to begin with. Shoot the arrow again several times to make sure that the results are consistent, and if the nock continues to be high and right, then choose a shaft with less spine. If the arrow sticks in the target fairly straight (the nock is high, but centered over the point of impact), it means the arrow is correctly spined and there's no need to shorten it any more. Shoot the arrow several times to confirm the results. If the arrow is correctly spined, then start gradually lowering the nocking point on the bowstring until the arrow hits fairly straight in the target.

If the nock of the arrow is high and to the left of the point of impact, then the arrow doesn't have enough spine. Shoot the arrow several more times to confirm, then shorten the arrow by $1/4$ inch and repeat the process. Continue the shooting and shortening process until the nock end of the arrow ends up roughly over the top of the point of impact every time, taking care not to shorten the arrow past the mark you made showing the minimum length.

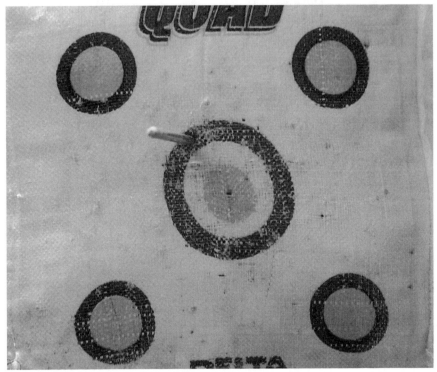

A properly tuned bare shaft should stick reasonably straight in a soft bag target.

Then, gradually lower the nocking point on the bowstring until the arrow shoots fairly straight without feathers. Once this is accomplished, write down all pertinent information, such as brace and nock heights, arrow length, and point weight for future use. Now, when you add feathers to the arrow, the shaft will recover from oscillation quickly and fly straight to the target. This will often tame any broadhead shooting problems you may have experienced in the past.

One last thing before moving on—before you shoot it, check every arrow for any damage that might result in a failure. I once shot a "perfectly good" wood shaft that broke when I released the bowstring and the back end of the arrow buried itself in the back of

Traditional bowhunters can choose among many excellent broadheads. Left to right: antique glue-on Bear Razorhead, modern Bear Razorhead, Zwickey Delta four-blade, Zwickey Eskimo two-blade, Ribtek glue-on, Ribtek with adapter, Razorcap three-blade, Wensel Woodsman three-blade glue-on, Wensel Woodsman with adapter, and Grizzly Grande with adapter.

my bow hand. An arrow goes through a lot of stress between the time you release the bowstring and the time you pull it from the target. These stresses cause wear, which can weaken the shaft material over time. Any arrows showing cracks or splinters should be discarded immediately. Also from time to time check your arrows for straightness by spinning them on the field point or rolling them across a flat surface. Any crooked ones should be used as kindling or tomato stakes.

Some Thoughts on Broadheads

If you stop and think about it, the arrow is the delivery system for the broadhead, the piece of equipment that actually does the work. Even if your arrow is perfectly tuned and your broadhead flies like laser beams straight to the target, it has to be capable of doing the job.

Many broadheads are found on the market today. Most are excellent, but some are very poor choices for the traditional bowhunter and should be avoided like the plague. Listen up because I'm only going to say this once: *Mechanical broadheads have no place in traditional bowhunting.* They may work fine for compound bows whose arrow speeds approach 300 feet per second, but if used with stickbows, mechanical broadheads use up precious kinetic energy during the process by which the blades are opened up. With traditional bows, a good two- or three-blade cut-on-contact broadhead will provide the best results. Stay away from replaceable blade broadheads whose tips must punch through hide rather than cut through, once again wasting kinetic energy. Tests conducted on deer hides with replaceable blade broadheads and cut-on-contact broadheads show that only 2 or 3 pounds of force is required for the cut-on-contact broadhead to slice through the hide while the replaceable blade broadhead requires 15 to 20 pounds of force to "punch" through the hide.

Some of the most widely used and time-proven broadheads for traditional bowhunters include two-blade offerings, resharpenable, reinforced, and tough as nails, made by Zwickey, Magnus, and Grizzly. Three-blade models, such as the Snuffer, Wensel Woodsman, and the Razorcap, are sharpened all the way to the tip and will begin cutting immediately without having to punch through the hide first. There are many more models on the market, but the ones listed above are tried and true and will serve you well.

Some of my favorite broadheads come with a tapered ferrule that is made to glue directly onto the end of a tapered wood shaft. A broadhead adapter glued into one of these broadheads allows the bowhunter to use these traditional broadheads with carbon and aluminum arrows as well. Be sure to do the math when assembling these components so that you maintain the same weight as the field points you used during bare shaft tuning. Any weight deviation will affect arrow spine and cause arrow flight problems, which will only be magnified by the broadhead. If you still experience flight problems with your broadheads even after properly tuning your arrows, a few tricks may help you work through them: Occasionally, turning a two-blade broadhead either horizontally or vertically will help arrow flight. Aligning a three-blade broadhead with the fletching can streamline the arrow enough to improve flight, and sometimes using a higher profile or longer fletching can stabilize broadheads better. Instead of a standard 5-inch right or left wing feather, try a high profile parabolic feather or a $5^1/2$-inch feather to straighten out your arrow flight more quickly. But keep in mind that it will slow your arrow down slightly.

Vented or non-vented broadheads also can make a difference. Vented blades, such as a Bear Razorhead or Magnus Snuffer, allow a crosswind to pass through and may improve the aerodynamics of your hunting arrow. On the other hand, you may find a solid broadhead, such as the Zwickey Eskimo, will do the trick. It's all a matter of finding what works best for you.

A sharp broadhead is obviously the best. There are many ways to resharpen a good traditional broadhead. A file is the most common sharpening tool, but Arkansas stones, crock sticks, and diamond hones also work very well. Sharpening a broadhead is like sharpening a hunting knife. Be sure to use an equal number of strokes on each edge to prevent changing the balance of the broadhead and to keep a constant angle as you hone. To maintain sharpness, always apply a dab of petroleum jelly to the edge once it's razor sharp. Even when not being used, a broadhead will dull due to oxidation that occurs with exposure to the elements. For this reason, constant touch-up is recommended to maintain the sharpness and efficiency of your broadhead. For in the field touch-ups, I carry a two-sided diamond hone with folding handles in medium and fine grits. It's small enough to fit in a pocket but big enough to

To sharpen broadheads, you can use a file, Arkansas stones, diamond hones, or carbide sharpeners set into a plastic handle to protect your fingers.

completely resharpen a broadhead. Plus, it doesn't require any sharpening medium for lubrication—just wipe it off on your pants leg and you're ready to go.

ACCESSORIES FOR TRADITIONAL BOWHUNTERS

Besides a **shooting tab or glove,** a few other accessories can help make you a better shot and a better traditional bowhunter. Take the **arm guard** for instance. A lot of traditional archers won't use an arm guard and claim it's not necessary if you use good shooting form. But a lot of traditional bowhunters, myself included, have botched a shot because the bowstring got caught on a bulky shirt-sleeve. While hunting, it's not always possible to get into the perfect position to make a shot and that bow arm can get a little closer to the string than it should. I find it always pays to wear some type of arm guard, if for no other reason than peace of mind. The arm guard doesn't have to be anything fancy as long as it performs the double task of keeping your sleeve out of the way and protecting your forearm from accidental string slap.

The **quiver,** another important accessory, is often overlooked as just a handy way to carry your arrows. Several good styles of quivers on the market work well for stickbow hunters, depending on your style of hunting. Back quivers, ranging from the old leather Howard Hill–style to the handy Catquiver line, are available with a variety of different pouches and even a fanny pack to carry extra gear. There is also the handy Bushmaster rotary quiver from Simmons Archery. Both the Catquiver and Bushmaster have the added advantage of providing protection for your fletching during wet weather or while in thick brush. If using a back quiver, keep in mind that it takes practice to get arrows in and out of the quiver quietly and without looking.

The hip quiver is another style that serves to carry arrows safely and securely. A good hip quiver will ride on the outside of your thigh and has a snap on the belt loop that allows you to take off the quiver without having to undo your belt. It should also have a deep puncture-proof broadhead cup to protect you and your broadheads. Hip quivers are handy if you don't like a bow or back quiver or if you carry a daypack or treestand on your back.

When I first began hunting with traditional bows many years ago, I carried my arrows in an old-fashioned back quiver, but after trying several different styles over the years, I finally settled on a universal strap-on style quiver that I could put on any of my bows. It carries five arrows securely (which is plenty) and stays fastened to my bow even after rough handling. In my opinion, the bow quiver is the handiest of all styles, regardless of what type of hunting I'm doing. The arrows are always at my fingertips, and I can

The three most common quivers for traditional bowhunters are (left to right) the bow quiver, the hip quiver, and the back quiver.

protect the fletching from the elements, if need be. Bow quivers can attach with rubber straps or grippers or bolt on to the side of the bow, if the bow is equipped with quiver bushings, or under the limb bolts on a takedown bow.

Pick your quiver according to how you hunt and how it will be used. I own at least one of each style and use all of them at some point during the year. Just make sure that the quiver you pick has quality arrow grippers and a puncture-proof hood and, if a bow quiver, mounts solidly and quietly to your bow. Don't end up like I did the year I bought a very cheap hip quiver from my archery

A soft case will protect your bow on short trips.

dealer and ended up having to retrace my steps back through the woods to find the arrows that had fallen out of it.

Another accessory a good traditional bowhunter can't be without is a **bow case.** Several options are available, depending on what your needs are. If you're driving a short distance to hunt, then a soft case provides adequate protection for your bow. But, if you're traveling on an airline or if you transport your bow in the back of the truck along with treestands and deer carts, you'll want something sturdier. I prefer the hard tube cases for longbows and the reinforced cases for recurves. Don't take chances with your stickbow. Why risk damaging your bow, when it could have easily been prevented?

Depending on how much gear you carry, you'll want to bring along a **fanny pack** or light daypack to avoid overstuffing your pockets. Fanny packs come in many styles, but I prefer one with a single large compartment. I carry little gear other than my mini survival kit and some bottles of water, and I like to position the compartment in front when I'm carrying a portable treestand on my back.

Whether a daypack (left), multicompartment fanny pack (center), or single-compartment fanny pack (right), a traditional bowhunter needs something to carry extra gear in.

Three items a bowhunter should never leave home without are a **spare bowstring,** a **bowstringer,** and a **spare shooting glove or tab.** Carry spares of everything and you can avoid the frustration of a trip back home. I don't know how many times I've arrived at my hunting area only to realize I've either lost or forgotten my shooting glove. I've also appreciated the spare string and bowstringer on those occasions when my bowstring accidentally came in contact with a sharp rock or a broadhead. To make sure I take everything with me I need, I've put together a brief bowhunter's checklist. I post this list in a conspicuous place prior to hunting season and use it to gather my supplies before each hunt. If you're forgetful like me, it will come in handy.

BOWHUNTER'S CHECKLIST
- Hunting license and tags
- Bow, quiver, and hunting arrows
- Spare bowstring and bowstringer
- Spare shooting tab or glove
- Mini survival kit
- GPS and/or compass, and maps
- Knife and field dressing gloves
- Sharpening device for knives and broadheads
- Grunt calls and rattling bag or antlers
- Scents
- Bow pull-up rope for treestand
- Face mask or headnet and gloves
- Hunter orange, when required

Take care when choosing and tuning your traditional tackle and put some thought into what works best for you. Stickbows and accessories are (and should be) a personal affair and should instill pride in the bowhunter. By the same token, don't become an "equipment junkie." It's not the bow or arrows as much as the archer behind them that truly makes a deadly traditional bowhunting combination. I know stickbow hunters who have spent a small fortune trying to find the "perfect" bow for them, one that would solve all their problems and turn them into the next Howard Hill. Unfortunately, it never did, and they could have saved that expense by instead concentrating on improving their hunting and instinctive shooting skill with the equipment they already had. Traditional archery and bowhunting are meant to be simple and satisfying activities. Spend time getting intimately acquainted with your equipment. Try it out under every conceivable condition and learn what it is capable of doing in your hands. Remember that *you* are the power and skill behind the bow, and the best bow in the world can't make a bad shooter any better.

Going afield with anything less than a properly tuned traditional bowhunting rig is not only irresponsible, but it will drastically decrease your chances of success in the whitetail woods. Likewise, if you fail to practice adequately and to hone your instinctive shooting skills to their utmost sharpness, you're hurting yourself and the sport of traditional bowhunting. The animals we pursue deserve our best, and we should never give them anything less.

- 2 -

Whitetails,
Inside and Out

The white-tailed deer is the favorite game animal of most traditional bowhunters across the United States. Making its home from southern Canada to Central America and Bolivia, the whitetail has continued to thrive, even in the face of adversity. Prolific, secretive, and challenging, whitetails are a natural match for modern-day traditional bowhunting, providing stickbow hunters with the ultimate test of their skills.

With a population estimated at around fourteen million in the United States alone, white-tailed deer have rebounded from the all-time lows they experienced in the late 1800s, when large-scale hunting and widespread clearing of land caused a radical drop in their numbers. At one time, the white-tailed deer outnumbered even the mighty buffalo and were a staple of both Native Americans and white settlers, who used the meat for food and the hides for clothing and trading. Thanks to wildlife management efforts, whitetails once again live in all but the most arid regions of our fifty states. Texas leads the country with around three and a half million deer, followed by Michigan, Pennsylvania, Wisconsin, and a few other states that boast deer populations exceeding a million animals.

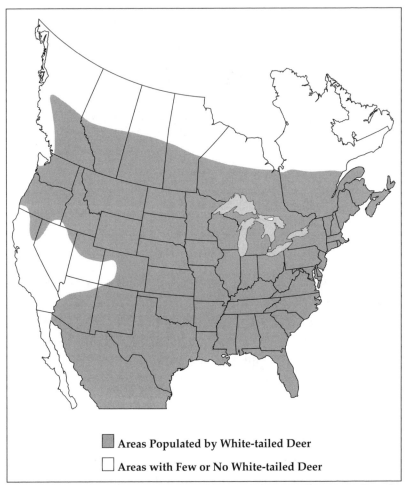

White-tailed deer inhabit all but a small part of the United States and southern Canada. There are even a few whitetails in Central America and Bolivia.

Although the physical characteristics of deer are affected by several factors, genetics and habitat have the most influence on their size. We've all seen pictures of gigantic deer taken regularly from the Canadian provinces and who hasn't dreamed of packing up our stickbows for a trip north to see for ourselves. Monstrous body size quite often makes the antlers of these deer look smaller than they really are. First-time bowhunters can easily be confused by this distortion and unknowingly allow a Pope and Young class deer to walk past without realizing how big those antlers really were.

The farther south you go, the smaller the average body size of the deer becomes. Antler size becomes more dependent on the genetics of the local herds; Texas and Mexico see their share of trophy-class animals with average body weights well below 200 pounds. But, even if you don't live in Canada, Texas, or Mexico, you may still get a crack at a big whitetail. A large buck has a habit of showing up in places where it's least expected, and that's one of the things I love the most about hunting white-tailed deer.

White-tailed bucks range from 125 pounds up to and over 300 pounds on the hoof. Does are smaller, averaging around 100 pounds, with a 130-pound doe a real trophy in most places. Adult whitetails range from about 62 inches to 86 inches in length from nose to rump. Although a deer can live to be fifteen years old, its average lifespan in the wild is only two to four years due to the many hazards it faces every day of its life.

Deer are ruminants, which means that they have a four-chambered stomach and chew their cud like a cow, allowing them to consume a large quantity of food at one time and digest it later. It also allows deer to better digest foods with low nutritional value, which is often necessary during hard winters and in areas with high deer populations. Deer normally bed down soon after eating their fill in order to chew their cud and this aids in the digestion process. After chewing for a period of time, the deer will reswallow the cud, which then goes to the second chamber of the stomach. Eventually the food passes through the third and fourth stomachs, still being digested and providing nutrients, before moving through the intestines and coming out in the pellet form we're all familiar with.

The breeding season of the whitetail occurs in November and December, depending on its geographic location, and usually lasts about one week. Once bred by a buck, a doe's pregnancy lasts about six and a half months, and its fawns will be born in early summer during the time of plenty. Does give birth to anywhere from one to three fawns, with twins being the average as long as the mother gets adequate nutrition during gestation. Biologists tell us that if a doe carrying twins isn't getting enough nutrition during the winter to safely carry both fawns, one fetus will actually absorb the other to lessen the demands on the mother's body and help ensure the birth of at least one healthy fawn.

After eight to ten weeks of nursing, the fawns are weaned and begin a full-time diet matching that of adult deer. The fawns stay with their mother until the following spring when the mother returns to her core area, and the family unit becomes less close-knit. A mature female often has a favorite fawning area that she will defend, even from members of her own clan. Other less dominant females must take whatever is left over. The young females will stay in the general area of their mother for their entire lives, but most of the buck fawns will leave instinctively to establish their own territories. If they don't, their mother will drive them away come fall. This prevents inbreeding but also partly, I suspect, keeps mature bucks from viewing her male offspring as competition and seriously injuring or killing him. White-tailed deer are sexually mature by age two, but I have seen mature white-tailed bucks chasing doe fawns during the rut when the competition for receptive females was high, making me wonder if perhaps some does don't come into estrous during their first year. As the breeding season moves along and more does become bred, bucks will often wander for miles in search of more receptive does to breed, often going without food and rest for long periods in order to satisfy the need to pass on their genes. Even bucks less than two and one-half years old will get caught up in the breeding ritual without fully understanding what's going on. Compare them to a teenage boy who is reaching puberty, and you'll see why these young bucks often respond well to calling and rattling techniques. Their curiosity, lack of understanding, and inexperience quite often lead to their downfall and make them the age class that most often ends up on the meat pole in hunting camp.

A buck's tendency to wander may account for those times when bucks that we've never seen before mysteriously appear in the middle of the rut. During early bow season, I often sight the same bucks over and over again on many different occasions, when I recognize them by their different physical characteristics. Then, as the rut comes into full swing, I spy one or two new bucks, quite often much bigger than the ones I'd previously seen who now seem to have disappeared. These sightings were normally preceded by an increase in both the size and number of rubs and scrapes that appeared in my hunting area. Perhaps these bucks had been there all along and were simply nocturnal until the rut compelled them to move during daylight hours, but experience and observation tell me that these bucks are from somewhere else and have come to this new area searching for receptive does.

A buck fawn is often referred to as a "button buck" because of the small bumps on his head where his antlers will eventually grow. By his second winter, he'll display a set of antlers that is usually a junior version of what he'll carry at maturity, but he may grow another point or two before reaching full maturity at three and one-half years. Bucks shed their antlers in January and February, with regrowth beginning in March. Deer antler grows exceptionally fast, at the rate of 1 to 2 inches per week with adequate nutrition, and these velvet-covered antlers will continue to develop until late August or early September, when the blood-rich velvet will die and fall off to be consumed by the buck for its protein content. Only then will the buck begin to rub his antlers on trees or take part in any sparring with other bucks. The rubs themselves are a known form of communication between deer, but I believe a buck rubs when the velvet first comes off simply to get the rest of the velvet and any remaining blood off his antlers so that pesky flies stop swarming around his head. I also believe this initial rubbing serves to polish the antlers and close up the pores in the bone. Have you ever seen how porous a buck's antlers are as soon as the velvet falls off? The texture is almost like chalk. Later on during the fall, the rubbing serves as both visual and olfactory signposts and helps to strengthen a buck's neck muscles for the eventual shoving matches with other bucks that he may encounter as the rut gets closer.

Many opinions exist on what causes a buck to have big antlers, but I believe a combination of genetics and nutrition allow a buck to reach his full potential. As a buck's antlers grow, his body robs calcium from his bones to facilitate growth in his rack. A deer that doesn't get adequate nutrition during the growth cycle will not reach his full potential, regardless of how good his father's genetics were. As for the genetics, well, I'm not a scientist, but I do believe that a buck will pass on certain genetic antler traits such as shape and number of points to his male offspring. On a nine hundred-acre farm I hunt frequently, I killed two different bucks, both two and a half years old with the same basic eight-point rack. Both deer had sticker points on the base of their antlers in the same locations, and both had racks that swept upward in an unusual manner. They also had matching drop tines growing off their left main beams. The kicker? I killed these bucks *three years apart*. The season after I killed the second of these bucks, I killed a grand old gray-faced monarch with a massive up-swept rack, sticker points at the base of his antlers, and, you guessed it, a drop tine growing off of his left main beam. Coincidence? I don't think so.

As expanding agriculture and urban sprawl have encroached on their woodland habitat, white-tailed deer have learned to co-exist in close proximity with humans. The more cities and suburbs grow, the more farmers must make use of every available parcel of land. As a result, the ground surrounding many metropolitan areas is planted with some type of crop, often right up to the edges of highly populated areas. White-tailed deer are caught in the middle. Yet as their habitat shrinks, their population continues to expand. Extremely adaptable, they have learned to live quite comfortably in city parks and on small suburban farms, often grazing in flowerbeds and gardens, much to the displeasure of those who did the planting. This population expansion also has resulted in an increase in car-deer accidents in both rural and urban areas. To deal with this deer explosion, many open-minded city and town councils have created urban white-tailed deer zones, where bowhunters are allowed to harvest whitetails in places where hunting was formerly prohibited. Hunting urban whitetails will be discussed in chapter 8.

White-tailed deer are creatures of the edge, preferring areas where heavy timber and open terrain come together, but I've seen whitetails in just about every type of environment imaginable. I once saw a trophy buck standing in the middle of a car dealership's lot at about 10 o'clock at night! This dealership was located next to a four-lane highway, directly between two wooded areas, one of which happened to be my favorite nine hundred-acre farm. Because it was the peak of the rut, I'm sure the buck was out look-ing for does and not a new car. But before I ever had the opportu-nity to get a shot at him, he was struck and killed by a truck while crossing that same highway a few nights later.

You may have heard it said that a white-tailed deer, like the Army, travels on its stomach. Many hunters agree with this state-ment, but I believe other factors also affect the movement of any deer. Common sense and years of experience and observation tell me that every time a deer moves, that movement is based on one of four physical influences. Seldom if ever will a deer wander without a pur-pose. It is moving to satisfy its hunger or thirst, find its bedding area, seek a mate, or flee from danger. Deer like undisturbed routine, and if allowed to follow its routine, a deer's movement can become pre-dictable. By becoming familiar with this routine and making sure he or she is in the right place at the right time, a traditional bowhunter can capitalize on this fact and seize the prize.

ANATOMY OF A WHITETAIL

For most traditional bowhunters, taking home meat doesn't necessarily describe a successful hunt, but let's be honest. The meat is the main reason we pursue game. Whitetails are fairly thin-skinned and easy to kill, as long as we place a razor-sharp broadhead in the location that will do the most damage.

The broadhead kills by hemorrhage, not by shock or trauma as a rifle bullet or slug does. Severing a major artery or shooting a broadhead through both lungs (pneumothorax) or the heart will cause rapid blood loss, shut off oxygen to the brain, and put any deer down quickly, often within a hundred yards. To put an arrow through a deer's vital zone, the traditional bowhunter must be proficient with his or her equipment, all of which should be well tuned. Proficiency will follow if a hunter practices correctly and constantly, which includes shooting broadheads regularly.

The vital zone is a fairly big target, about 10 inches by 12 inches in size, contained within the deer's chest cavity, where it is protected by the deer's ribs. Depending on the size of the deer, the vital zone runs vertically from about 6 inches below the top of the back down to about 4 inches above the bottom of the chest. Horizontally, it runs from a spot beneath the shoulder blade to where the diaphragm is connected to the ribcage. The only obstacle to reaching the vital zone is the deer's shoulder blade, although a heavy arrow and sufficient draw weight will provide adequate penetration. To avoid the shoulder blade, simply do not to hit it in the first place. A broadside or quartering away shot is the best shot to take on any game animal, but this requires the bowhunter to place an arrow where it needs to go. When the deer is quartering away, it opens up the vital zone to allow a broadhead to slip cleanly behind the shoulder blade and penetrate deeply into the chest cav-

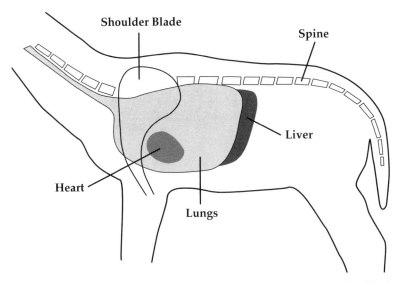

The deer's heart and lungs, its vital zone, are protected by the shoulder blade and ribs.

ity. When shooting at a broadside deer, wait until the leg closest to you is forward; this allows the shoulder blade to slide forward, thus opening up the chest cavity. Be cautious on any extreme quartering away shots because the vital zone will become narrower as the angle increases. Not only does this cut down on the size of the target, but it increases the likelihood that the arrow will become buried in the offside shoulder, preventing an exit wound and leaving a sparse blood trail, which makes tracking difficult.

Several years ago, I read an article that compared the vital zone on a white-tailed deer to a basketball. The writer said that if you visualized the vital zone of the whitetail as a basketball in the middle of its chest, you could shoot an arrow through the middle of the basketball from **any** angle and get a killing shot. Wrong, wrong, wrong.

To make a quick kill and prevent needless suffering of the game animal, the traditional bowhunter should consider the broadside

The size of the vital zone shrinks on an extreme quartering away angle.

and quartering away shots as the **only** two acceptable shot scenarios, no matter how big the deer's antlers are or how badly the hunter wants to kill the deer. Any other shot runs a high risk of causing the deer injury but not death, something you don't want to have to live with. Sure, we've all heard stories of shots taken on a deer facing either head-on or directly away from the bowhunter (a.k.a. the "Texas Heart Shot") and the animal eventually dying and being recovered, but were the shots good or just plain luck? I can tell you this, such shots were bad decisions, definitely *not* ethical, and the bowhunters who made those shots had no regard for the animal they were hunting. The old saying "I'd rather be lucky than good" has no place in the world of white-tailed deer hunting or in the mouth of a traditional bowhunter. Although this isn't a book about ethics, I like to think that traditional bowhunters hold themselves to a high moral and ethical level while hunting. Perhaps it's because we choose to hunt with gear that requires a higher level of skill and commitment than those who need sights, high-speed compound bows, and range finders to accomplish their goals.

BOWHUNTING PRACTICE FOR THE WHITETAIL SEASON

I love to shoot traditional bows, and I'm sure you feel the same way. When it comes to practicing for the upcoming deer season, nothing beats some serious practice with a realistic three-dimensional deer target. Shooting your traditional bow at a live animal is not the same as punching holes in a bull's-eye on the face of a bag target, or shooting at the outline of a deer's vital zone printed on heavy stock paper, but 3-D target practice does give you feedback on where your shot would have struck a live animal. I prefer 3-D targets that have the internal anatomy of a whitetail outlined on the side of the target in exactly the same place it would be on a live animal. There's no lying to yourself when you walk up to the target and realize that, if this would have been a live animal and your shot was anywhere except the vitals, you would have had a long tracking job and maybe even lost the animal. That's why (and you'll hear this again) it's important to take your practice seriously and only shoot one arrow at a time, as though you were shooting at a live animal in a hunting environment.

When choosing a 3-D target, get one made of high-quality materials that will withstand a lot of use. Quality targets, like the ones made by McKenzie, will outlast the cheaper versions two to one, saving you money in the long run. Also select a brand that offers a replaceable midsection instead of just the small replacement vital zone. Eventually the area surrounding the small replaceable vital zone will wear out, too, making the target unusable. Keep

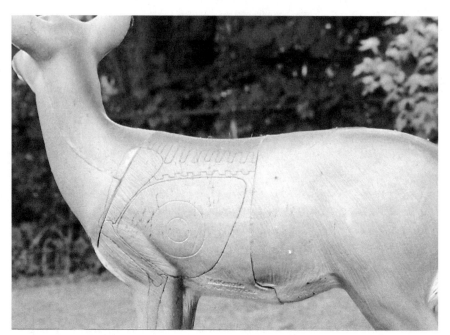

There's no question about where your arrow would have struck a live deer when you use a 3-D target that outlines anatomical structure. This one shows the spine, shoulder blade, and leg bones.

your 3-D target out of the weather, especially direct sunlight as UV light will cause the foam to deteriorate rapidly. For minor repairs and quick fixes, pick up a kit containing ingredients and dyes that let you mix your own matching filler material.

When practicing, set up your hunting bow with everything that you'll have when the season starts, including a bow quiver, if you use one. Pre-season practice is the time to get used to shooting your bow with the quiver on it. If you're like me, once deer season is over, the bow quiver comes off and is replaced with a back quiver so I can carry a lot of arrows while I'm at the range. You can count on the bow feeling different in your hand once the bow quiver is attached. It changes the overall balance, especially if you hunt with a bow that has little mass to start with, such as the little Fox

Archery longbow I prefer. My hunting quiver (a Great Northern strap-on) filled with hunting arrows weighs more than the longbow itself.

Also when practicing for deer season, keep in mind that what you wear on the range in warm weather is a lot different than what you wear in the field under cooler conditions. Bulky clothing, gloves, and headnets can affect your shooting accuracy, so you should practice in your hunting clothes before the season starts. All these things may seem trivial, but when you come face-to-face with a deer, you'll want to be able to concentrate on making that shot without having to worry about all the little things that could go wrong. As I like to say, control the "controllables."

Shooting from a treestand or the inside of a ground blind requires practice. Both of these hunting techniques are highly productive, yet few hunters take the time to practice from what they'll be hunting from come deer season. Shooting down at an animal from a stand requires the shooter to bend forward at the waist instead of just lowering the bow arm. Simply lowering the bow arm changes the instinctive sight picture dramatically and will cause you to shoot either too high or too low. Try to maintain correct shooting form as you bend at the waist and always "aim" a little low when shooting down.

Shooting from inside a ground blind also makes a difference in your sight picture, especially if you hunt from a fully enclosed blind that is dark on the inside. Not only are you standing in deep shadow and trying to shoot at a target in bright sunlight, but have to shoot through a small window and overcome the added distraction of the tent walls in your peripheral vision. Sitting in a blind for an extended period of time can really mess with your depth perception. Before the season begins, take the time to set up your blind and practice shooting at a 3-D target from inside it. I find that my depth perception seems to suffer when shooting past 10 yards, and I always think the deer is farther away than it really is.

Bend at the waist instead of lowering the bow arm when shooting from a treestand.

The same can be said when shooting at a deer standing in cover rather than in the open. When you shoot at a deer that's standing in cover, such as in the woods, the ground cover between you and the deer allows your subconscious "computer" to better estimate range and tell your bow arm how high to elevate to get the arrow to fly just right. But when that same deer is standing in an open field, with only grass between the two of you, your brain has a more difficult time judging the distance without any reference points between your eyes and the target. Practice both scenarios from your treestand or ground blind to make sure you'll be ready when a shot presents itself.

For still-hunting practice, I like to set up my 3-D target in a variety of situations and "practice" my stalking and approach before taking a shot. I also take several shots (one arrow at a time) from several different broadside and quartering away positions, varying the distance on each shot until I feel comfortable with my shooting.

One of the best ways to prepare for a season of still-hunting is to attend a 3-D archery tournament. These tournaments are popping up all over the place, and most of them offer classes that set up bowhunters with shots at ethical distances, given the constraints of traditional equipment. Besides enjoying the camaraderie of shooting with fellow traditionalists, you can practice shooting in different terrains and environments, all while adhering to the important practice principal of only taking one shot at a time. Many of these 3-D events also have "warm-up" shoots prior to the upcoming deer season that feature all 3-D deer targets instead of the normal mixture of different species. I try to attend one or two of these events in late summer, just to get ready for the real thing, and I always find them valuable for working out the kinks and making sure my bowhunting rig is ready for the season. One word of advice—if your local 3-D tournament host is built around the compound crowd and doesn't cater to traditional archers (i.e., they don't have classes for traditional shooters or the stakes are too far from the target), find another traditionalist and attend anyway. When you go to shoot, ignore the stakes and take the shot from what is a realistic and ethical range for you. Then, throw your scorecard in the trash as you leave. I guarantee that not only will you enjoy it, but it will benefit you in the fall.

I can't stress this enough: The closer you can make your bow-hunting practice to a real hunting situation, the less likely that you will make a mistake when the time comes to shoot at a live white-tailed deer. As a police officer and veteran of the U.S. Army infantry, I often hear the saying, "Train like you fight, fight like you train." For traditional bowhunters, this phrase can be reworked to say, "Practice like you hunt, hunt like you practice."

To become a proficient traditional bowhunter, you must practice correctly *and* often. I shoot fifty to one hundred arrows from my longbow every day, come rain, sun, wind, or snow. As long as my attitude and concentration are there, I know I'll have a productive practice. My bow is set up exactly as it is when I go hunting, and although I may not necessarily wear my hunting clothes, I do wear clothing that is similarly restrictive, along with a headnet and gloves. I use correct shooting form, concentrate on every shot, and shoot a single arrow as though a live animal were in front of me. After I shoot that arrow, I go to the target and evaluate the shot, determining whether or not it would have done the job. Shooting one arrow at a time is critical not only because that's usually all you will shoot at a live deer, but it also keeps you from ruining arrows by stacking them too close together. Instead of concentrating on the arrows already sticking in the target, you can pick a spot to focus your single shot. Only practice when you're mentally prepared, both to avoid frustration and to prevent yourself from picking up bad habits in your shooting form that will affect your accuracy.

When shooting at my 3-D target, I use field points rather than broadheads. Regardless of how durable and how many broadhead shots the manufacturer claims its target can withstand, broadheads will cause massive damage. I've correctly tuned my bowhunting rig so that my broadhead arrows fly the same and hit in the same spot as my field points. To practice with my broadheads on a regular basis, I use a separate foam target. When the season arrives, I have no doubts that both my equipment and I are in top form, and my confidence level lets me picture that arrow burying itself behind the deer's shoulder before I ever take the shot.

White-tailed deer hunting is more than a hobby or sport for most of us. It's a way of life. Learning everything I can about my favorite quarry not only makes me a better hunter, it helps me appreciate the animal when I see it in the wild. Every traditional bowhunter should make it a point to learn the anatomy of the white-tailed deer. I recommend visiting the National Bowhunter Education Foundation's website (www.nbef.org) and go to the whitetail anatomy and shot placement guide. Download it, print it, and study it until you can look at a live deer and visualize where every organ is. I also recommend reading *The Perfect Shot/Mini-Edition For North America* by Craig Boddington. Although this book is written primarily for firearms hunters and covers other North American game in addition to the white-tailed deer, the traditional bowhunter will find the illustrations showing the vital zone of the whitetail from several different angles invaluable.

Killing a deer is not an act that should be undertaken lightly or with poor preparation. Your sense of joy and accomplishment in the hunt should be tempered with appreciation and perhaps a touch of regret as you realize the mortality of all living things. The whitetail is a majestic animal, full of life and deserving of both our respect and our best effort as traditional bowhunters. Let's not give them anything less.

- 3 -

Scouting and Mapping Techniques

A consistently successful white-tailed deer hunter knows that many things have to occur before the butcher knife can be sharpened. For starters, to kill a deer with the traditional bow and arrow, you must be close enough to your prey to obtain a good unobstructed shot. The deer must be reasonably calm and preferably standing still. Although the nation's whitetail population is high and deer can be found in many unexpected places, their sheer numbers are not enough to guarantee backstraps on the grill.

Creatures of habit, deer will spend 90 percent of their time in 30 percent of a given area, as long as their routine goes relatively undisturbed. Your best chance for being in the right place at the right time is to study the deer's habits, learn their routines, and select a certain *area* to still-hunt, a specific *tree* in which to place your treestand, or a particular *spot* for a blind. Each of these specific locations will depend upon what the deer are doing during a particular time of year. So, to be a successful deer hunter, you must not only know your hunting area inside and out, but you have to know your local deer population and the general habits of white-tailed deer.

Whitetails frequent edges, such as where a brush field meets an open wooded area.

Deer are creatures of the edge, preferring areas where changes in landscape and terrain come together. Because, like most people, deer prefer to take the path of least resistance, areas where thick brush meets open fields will often show signs of deer travel. Saddles (the low area between two hilltops) are often good places to hunt because deer not only use the low area for cover, but they prefer the easier route of walking between the hilltops rather than over them. Benches (flat shelves that run alongside ridges) are good places to check for deer sign, especially when the ridge tops are covered with mast trees, including oaks that produce the acorns that whitetails love so dearly. Look for locations in your hunting area where two woodlots are connected by a thin band of trees or an overgrown fencerow. Any of these areas are conducive to deer hunting and should be the first things you look for when scouting a location for the first time.

Three factors shape the behavior and routine of the white-tailed deer: food (including water when it's hot out), bedding areas, and relative safety. If deer have abundant food, a safe place to bed, and are relatively unmolested, they tend to stay put. What they eat depends upon what time of year it is. In the spring and summer, during times of plenty, deer will feed just about anywhere and bed in just about any thicket. This time of plenty usually includes early bow season and, depending on your geographic location, continues through to the end of October. Depending on where you live and what your hunting area consists of, deer will eat standing crops, green browse, and mast.

Deer have their favorite foods, but they will eat them in the proper order to get the best nutritional value. Deer love soybeans, from the time the plant first comes up until the bean pods sprout. Once the beans appear, the plants become less tasty and lose a lot of their nutritional value. Deer don't care too much for the leaves and stalks after they turn brown, but I have seen crowds of deer feeding in the chaff thrown out behind the combine as the beans were being picked. As soon as the combine drew near, the deer would run back to the edge of the field, only to return to the chaff after the combine passed by.

Corn, on the other hand, is usually preferred after the kernels have hardened on the cob. In fact, deer will actually bed right in the cornfield after the crop has matured, since it provides them with both food and cover. One of my favorite activities is to ride the corn picker around the field to observe what deer come running out.

At first glance, crop fields may seem like the perfect place to hunt, but they're extremely seasonal and often are difficult to hunt with any kind of consistency, especially when deer can enter the field from any direction. Deer usually visit these wide-open fields when it's dark, staging in certain areas, such as oak groves, before moving into the crop fields to feed and socialize. These staging

Crop fields are great places to hunt, but deer can enter the field from lots of places. Only careful scouting can tell you where to hang a stand.

areas are usually secondary food sources, and deer will linger there and snack on acorns as they wait for the cover of darkness.

WHY BOTHER SCOUTING?

Quite simply, if you don't scout, then you don't know when, where, how, and why deer are using a particular area. Without scouting, hunting would be nothing more than sticking a treestand in any old tree in hopes that a deer will walk by or strolling aimlessly along through the woods hoping to run into a deer. Scouting can give you an overall view of the big picture, *if* you do it correctly. I don't know how many times while scouting, that I've ended up finding a place just begging to be hunted. Usually it's a spot where I haven't bothered to look before simply because previously I had dismissed it as not good enough to devote time to.

Take the time late one year when I was bowhunting for squirrels after I had filled my deer tags. I was ambling along, looking and enjoying myself, when I spooked a doe. She ran down into a drainage surrounded by the thickest vegetation you could imagine. Wondering why she chose to run that direction when she could have taken a much easier course, I walked to the edge of the draw and spied a well-worn deer trail going through the bramble. Walking down to where she had disappeared, I slipped easily through the thick stuff and entered into a whole new world, just ripe with deer sign. Several hundred yards later, I came out at the far edge of what used to be an overgrown apple orchard before it became a pasture for black angus cattle. This wide valley, which I had never taken time to explore, was hidden on all sides by nasty thick blowdowns and briar tangles, which led me to mistakenly believe that it was worthless for deer hunting. Since my discovery, I have taken many deer from that little place, which I have come to call the "New World."

SCOUTING TIPS

Scouting of any kind is best done from a distance, the farther away from the hunting area, the better. Because few intrusions into the world of the whitetail go unnoticed, binoculars are your best friend. Miniature binoculars may work during the hunt, but you will need a full-size set of optics for your scouting. The more powerful the optics, the better they'll serve you. However, if like me, you can't afford a nine hundred dollar pair of binoculars, get yourself a cheaper full-size set of 10x50s, such as Bushnell sells. That particular magnification has the best combination of light-gathering ability and clarity for the price and will serve you well while scouting your whitetail hunting areas. Since they'll be used in all kinds of weather conditions, make sure you get optics that are waterproof and fogproof, if possible. Also invest in a comfortable padded neck strap to avoid the sheer weight of the binoculars from becoming literally a pain in the neck.

Long-distance scouting keeps your scent out of the hunting area and is the best way to prevent changing deer behavior patterns.

When scouting, begin at the outskirts of your hunting area and observe as much as you can of your landscape before moving in to confirm your information. About two months before the season opens, I carefully check the field edges at dusk and dawn, scanning for deer activity and noting where deer enter or exit the field. Later on when my scouting becomes more intense, I'll go back to check these areas again. Other great scouting locations for daylight are hilltops and field edges, which are far enough from suspected areas of deer use to keep from contaminating them, yet close enough to allow me to tell what's going on.

I like to make a map of each of my hunting areas. Using colored pencils and several sheets of typing paper taped together, I draw as much detail as I can, including open fields, crop fields, fence lines, draws, and saddles. Then, I begin recording information on this map from each scouting trip. Every time I see a deer, I will record

While compact binoculars (left) are good for hunting, full-size optics such as these 10x50s are better for scouting.

the location of the sighting on my map, as well as the time of day, the sex of the animal, and its direction of travel. If I see a doe, for instance, I'll make a "D" draw a line through it with an arrow pointing in the direction the doe was traveling. I'll also record the date and time of day, general weather conditions (including prevailing wind direction), and anything else I think is important.

Once you have quite a few "Ds" and "Bs" on your map, it's time to put the map to work for you. Start by extending the lines you drew through the letters all the way to the edges of the paper in both directions. Do this very lightly so as not to make a mess of your map. Once you've done this, look for where the lines intersect. I call these areas "hubs." Look carefully at the hubs, especially locations where several lines intersect. Are they close to any actual terrain feature or areas of high deer traffic that you're already familiar with? You may discover later on that some of these hubs are

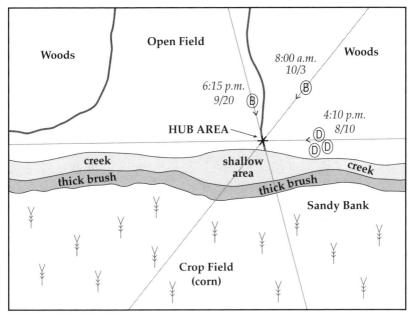

Draw a map of your hunting area with as much detail as possible, and log your deer sightings accurately to find the hubs or intersections of deer paths.

located near previously undiscovered "hot spots" such as a fence crossing or saddle. Once you discover how these hubs will point you to locations where deer pass by regularly, you'll understand why these maps are such a valuable tool.

Topographical Maps and Satellite Photographs—Scout from Home
Scouting an area sounds great, you say, but where do I start when scouting a new spot and what do I do if my scouting time is limited? How can I be sure that I'm separating likely deer haunts from places that probably wouldn't support a flock of sparrows? Don't despair. You can prescout an area and get a reasonable idea of where to hunt without ever setting foot on the property simply by looking at aerial or satellite photographs and topographical maps of the area you're interested in. Both are available from several places. On the Internet, a website called Terraserver offers satellite pictures,

and the U.S. Geological Service provides detailed topographical maps. The valuable information gleaned from these laminated maps and satellite photos makes them well worth the cost.

Before using photos and maps, you will need to know how to read a topographical map. Topographical maps are generally covered with squares, the size of which is determined by the scale used. A topographical map in a 1:24,000 scale, for instance, means that one unit on the map equals 24,000 units of actual ground. Those units are usually inches. So, 1 inch on the map will equal 24,000 inches or 2,000 feet on the ground. The map also contains contour lines, which identify such terrain features as hilltops, ridges, and saddles, all areas frequently used by deer. The closer the contour lines are together on the map, the steeper the elevation. A legend at the bottom of the map explains many of the symbols shown on the map face. With a little study, you can learn to read topographical maps quite easily.

Satellite photos are exactly that, pictures of an area taken by an orbiting satellite. I like to go on the various websites and, by following the instructions, navigate my way to the photographs that cover my hunting area. (I've even found satellite photos of my home.) These photos are extremely useful when you have a large chunk of land to hunt on. You can see what's on the land and how it's laid out before actually setting foot on it.

If you place the topographical map next to the satellite photo of the same area, you will obtain a complete picture of the hunting area, almost in 3-D. By poring over those satellite photos, you can identify potential hunting areas. For example, let's say you're interested in hunting a huge tract of public land and you want to find an area with a high probability of producing deer. Most hunters on public land don't want to venture too far away from their vehicles to hunt, and only the most dedicated will travel into areas that are difficult to get to. By looking at a satellite picture of the area, you can pick out potential hunting locations based on what we know white-tailed deer need to live, thrive, and survive. We'll talk more about hunting public ground in chapter 6.

One of the first things I look for when examining pictures of new hunting areas are food sources, especially crop fields that are close to public hunting ground. Crop fields are usually easy to identify because they're open and sectioned off from the surrounding areas. If the satellite photo was taken when the crops were in the ground, you can easily identify them by the planted rows. If you happen to spot a crop field on the back side of public hunting ground, you've found a good place to hunt, provided nobody else has gone to the same trouble you have. Remember, the harder a spot is to get to, the less likely somebody else is going to hunt there and the more likely deer will be found as long as the area provides them with what they need.

Once you've located likely areas on the topographical map, take your maps and satellite photographs and go explore the area on foot. I try to accomplish this as early in the year as possible; January and February are the best months for scouting because deer movement can still be found in the woods. Once you're at the spots, try to figure out what in the area would attract deer. Determining whether it's a seasonal food source, a staging area, or a travel corridor between food sources and bedding areas will help you decide when and how you hunt the area.

Traditional bowhunters often like to do things the hard way, but there's no shame in using a little modern technology to help you with your scouting. Once you get a feel for the topographical maps and satellite photographs, you will learn to see the big picture and will gain a greater understanding of the area you hunt. I even use these resources for familiar areas that I've hunted for many years.

THE BIG THREE
Whitetail hunting season can be broken down into three distinct "mini-seasons," each of which has its own way of helping us to

decide where to hunt. By their very description, the pre-rut, rut, and post-rut tell us what the deer are doing. When changes occur in the deer's behavior or to affect their food sources or safe bedding areas, our hunting plan must shift to get us back on track with the deer's habits and routine. Occasional scouting during the season will be required. Your scouting can be either passive, which means simple observation and note taking while you're hunting, or aggressive, where you go out in the field to actually get a handle on deer movement. Aggressive scouting is what we do before hunting season starts.

Pre-Rut Scouting

The pre-rut season begins opening day and runs until about the third week of October, with overlap occurring depending on geographical location. At this warmer time of year, deer are the easiest to pattern, yet their noctural movement makes it difficult to connect with them during legal hunting hours.

During the pre-rut time of plenty, deer are feeding leisurely on mast crops, corn, soybeans, and oats. Fawns are nearly weaned and are feeding mostly on the same vegetation as the adults. Bucks are in bachelor groups and will spar a little now and then to determine their hierarchy. As long as their routine remains undisturbed, deer will bed as close to their food source as possible.

If you're intimately familiar with your hunting area, finding deer during this season will be easy. Most of the deer activity will occur right before dark and in the early morning hours, and your job will be to identify the main feeding spots for the whitetails in your particular area. If crop fields are available, post yourself at a distance and, using your binoculars, observe the activity and make careful notes about time, the sex and number of deer, and the locations where they entered the feeding area. The more often you do this, the better and more complete your understanding of their routine will be. This observation system will apply to any open area frequented by deer on a regular basis, as long as you can observe from a safe distance.

If the deer in your area are deep-woods deer that don't feed regularly in open fields, then your scouting job is a bit harder. Here's where past experience about an area comes in handy. Start by drawing a map of the area and then use your memory to record deer sightings on the map from years past. Also record any areas within the woods, such as groves of oak trees, where you know the deer congregate to feed.

Once you have an idea of where the deer are feeding, it's time to identify where they bed. Favorite bedding areas in the warmer months include cool, dense areas with thick vegetation that still allow deer to watch for danger. These can include honeysuckle thickets, tall patches of weeds, or low-growing vegetation in shady areas. Common sense and prior experience are the best teachers here. Going in and physically searching for bedding areas may spook the deer and cause them to seek a different place to bed. Remember, if you find an area that's littered with deer droppings, then you've found a bedding area. The first thing deer usually do after bedding down is to relieve themselves to make room for the food they'll digest while bedded.

Once you've nailed down the bedding and feeding areas, it's time to move in a little closer and find a good ambush location. Make this a quick in-and-out scouting trip, where you simply locate and verify trails, travel corridors, and other areas that might make good hunting spots. This is also the time to hang any lock-on stands and to clear shooting lanes. This preseason scouting trip is best taken during the midday, when deer are bedded and less likely to be encountered. Start in the areas where you've seen the deer feed and work backwards, trying to find their travel routes from feeding to bedding locations. Keep in mind that, during this early season, deer usually wait until the last minute of daylight to come out in the open fields to feed. However, they often congregate in the woods around oak trees and other secondary food sources while waiting for the cover of darkness. If you can, take advantage of this earlier movement in the afternoon when hunting hours are legal. Knowing the locations of secondary feeding areas is vital, because later on when their food in the fields has been depleted, these food sources will become primary locations for hungry deer.

The key to preseason scouting is stealth and making sure that you don't do anything to change the habits and routines of the deer you'll be hunting. Conduct as much of your observation as possible from long distance with your binoculars. Make only one or two forays into the woods before the season starts, and never venture into suspected bedding areas. The careful notes you make on your map now will serve you well throughout the season.

Scouting during the Rut

This book isn't about trophy hunting, but let's face it—we all want to see big bucks. I don't know a single traditional bowhunter who would pass up a wallhanger. If big bucks are your thing, you'll most likely get your chance during the "rut."

The beginning of the rut depends on your geographical location. In most northern states, it begins in early November and lasts a couple of weeks. In the South, it may not begin until sometime in December, but it usually runs all the way into January. If you're willing to invest the time and money, you could even chase rutting bucks from north to south in several states for a period of three months.

One of the things I enjoy most about this time of year is seeing bucks I've never observed before, especially during the heat of the rut. White-tailed does don't come into estrous all at once, so bucks will sometimes travel long distances in search of a hot doe, forsaking food and rest for propagation of the species.

Although I'm not a huge fan of hunting over buck sign, I will use rubs and scrapes to help locate a buck's core area and determine his route of travel. The size of the track in a scrape can tell you the body size of the buck that made it, but it won't tell you the size of his antlers. Large rubs can. There's an old saying that goes, "Big bucks and little bucks both rub little trees, but only big bucks rub big trees." When examining rubs, I look for gouge marks in the tree made by brow tines. How deep and far apart they are can sometimes be an indicator of antler size, but not always. The best indicator of a buck's size is how big he looks when you see him.

Volumes have been written about how to hunt big white-tailed bucks. Such methods as scrape hunting secrets, hunting a rub line, and calling and rattling are hit and miss in my opinion. If you really want to kill a big buck, you have to find the doe's hangout. Although a buck will travel outside his home range during the rut, a white-tailed doe won't. She'll remain in her home area and let the bucks look for her.

If you've been keeping your map up to date during the pre-rut, you've probably seen more does than bucks. Remember those hub areas we talked about? Now is the time to hunt them. Hub areas will attract bucks looking to find receptive females. It's the equivalent of a carload of teenage boys cruising the local drive-in. The bucks will stay on the downwind side of the area, scent checking each doe from a distance until he finds one that's in estrous.

Sometimes hub areas will actually consist of intersecting trails. Subordinate bucks may use these same trails looking for females, but you can bet the older, wiser bucks won't. Instead, they will keep to the downwind side and use their nose to help locate a doe in heat. Inspection of the downwind side of these major trails and intersections will often reveal the presence of a much fainter trail, one made by cruising bucks. These faint trails can also be located downwind of major scrape lines and bedding areas used by groups of females.

Scouting at this time should still occur at a distance, because if a big buck thinks you're after him, the game is over. Continue to use your binoculars whenever possible and keep your map updated. You may want to start a new map at this time to record buck sightings and locations of rub and scrape lines. The rubs and scrapes themselves don't excite me, but I like what they can tell me when I put all the information together on my map.

Post-rut Scouting

Hunting after the rut, when the chasing is over and the deer have settled back down to their normal routines, is a good time to put meat in the freezer. During this time, the weather can be foul, and what had been a highly productive area may now be void of any appreciable deer activity. The key to hunting whitetails after the weather turns bad is, once again, food sources. Depending on the severity of the winter in your hunting location, deer may be reduced to feeding on greenbriar and other woody browse.

Remember the "secondary" food sources you looked for during the pre-rut when the deer congregated before moving out into the open fields to feed? These have now become primary food sources, provided anything remains after squirrels and wild turkeys have had their share. By this time of year, the deer are often weary and skittish after weeks of being chased by hunters bearing both bows and firearms. They will often seek out locations to bed and feed where they feel safe. Scouting for food sources during the post-rut when food may be sparse requires a bit more work. Once again, be cautious while scouting since deer at this edgy time will tolerate little or no pressure before becoming nocturnal. Look for out-of-the-way areas where food and secure bedding cover are in close proximity to one another.

TRAIL TIMERS AND SCOUTING CAMERAS

Scouting is an important part of deer hunting, and nothing can take its place. No amount of gear, gadgets, or new technology will make that whitetail magically appear in front of you. The only thing more important than good, thorough scouting of your intended hunting areas is proficiency with your traditional bow.

Before I close on the subject of scouting, take note that I've made no mention whatsoever of trail timers or scouting cameras. Quite simply, I don't think they are worth the cost. Trail timers are simple digital clocks that are rigged by placing a trip wire across a suspected deer trail and then connecting the trip wire to the clock. When something strikes the trip wire, a stop pin pulls out of the digital clock to record the exact time and date of the disturbance. More advanced trail timers are triggered by infrared and will record multiple events. Since anything could have activated the timer, from a falling tree limb to a low-flying bird, a wild turkey, or a dog, the effectiveness of a trail timer is limited.

Scouting cameras, on the other hand, will tell you exactly what came by on the trail, but they still only give you a picture of a particular millisecond in time. What you'll have is a picture of a single animal that may or may not pass by that location again. A single occurrence in a single location amounts to absolutely no information that you can make real use of. If you like taking wildlife photos without actually having to be there, or if you just want to try to get a picture of a particular animal you've seen in a certain area, then the scouting camera may be for you, but stop and think about this. Most of the time the camera will use a flash to ensure adequate lighting for a good picture. You may have heard that deer are used to seeing lightning and a bright flash won't bother them. Hogwash. Deer are not stupid. No trip into the white-tailed deer's world goes unnoticed, and if you're making multiple trips to the same spot to retrieve film or to download files from a digital camera, sooner or later the deer are going to figure out that those bright flashes are connected to the human odor in the area and they'll change their behavior accordingly. I believe that the little information you'll gain from these cameras is just not worth the possibility of ruining a good hunting area, especially when you can obtain more information with less risk by putting forth a little effort on your own.

- 4 -

Stalking and Still-hunting Whitetails

Still-hunting: The act of moving with stealth through the hunting environment in an attempt to locate a game animal to stalk.

Stalking: The stealthy movement involved when a game animal has been spotted and the hunter is attempting to intercept the animal and get a shot.

With the invention of the treestand, many whitetail hunters have all but given up stalking and still-hunting, unless it's to or from their stand. That's a shame, especially since a lot of prime whitetail habitat can't be hunted from a treestand. To me, moving quietly through the woods, stickbow in hand, is the essence of deer hunting. It brings to mind images of Native Americans slipping from shadow to shadow with a sturdy selfbow in hand and a pelt quiver filled with carefully crafted arrows tipped with razor-sharp stone heads.

For hundreds of years, bowhunters have taken game successfully and consistently with this method. To harvest a white-tailed deer, whether a buck or a doe, from the ground is an accomplishment to be proud of. It is not an easy feat. Whitetails have an almost uncanny sense of their surroundings, and they usually know you're there long before you even see them. As a matter of fact, for the number of deer that we see while stalking and still-hunting, I'd be afraid to guess how many more have seen us first and simply disappeared without us ever knowing they were there.

To get a shot at a deer on the deer's own terms, we must avoid detection long enough to get within the range of our traditional tackle. Deer have three senses that work against us: hearing, sight, and smell. Of those three, the sense of smell is the hardest to fool. Even with all of the products on the market designed to hide us from a deer's nose, we can't contain all of our odor. Deer have excellent eyesight, but their visual acuity is based on movement. Stand still wearing drab-colored hunting clothes, and they might not even see you. As to their hearing, any sound out of the ordinary concerns them. A metallic rattle, a muffled cough, or the squeak of rubber or leather will get their attention. When hunting on the ground, try to control as many of the "controllable" factors as you can. Before we get started on the basics of stalking and still-hunting, let's talk about those controllable factors.

SCENT

What with even high-dollar clothing on the market claiming to hide you from a deer's nose, I believe that our search for scent-control products is getting way out of hand. I'd rather spend my money on some new shafts or broadheads, but the choice is yours. Just remember, most everybody you see endorsing these expensive products is compensated for the endorsement. I'm not saying that these products *don't* work to some degree, but I'm not sure they *do* either. If you do use scent-blocking clothing of any kind, just keep in mind that by wearing it you are not suddenly invisible to the deer's nose. Enough scent will escape to alert a whitetail to your presence. However, you can further reduce your scent by paying attention to what you do before you ever get dressed. That means developing some kind of scent-eliminating routine that starts at home.

A few of the scent-control products I use include (left to right) Scent-A-Way body soap and shampoo by Hunter's Specialties; Scent Killer clothing and equipment spray by Wildlife Research Center; Sport-Wash laundry detergent by Sno Seal; and Vanishing Hunter scent eliminator by Hawg's Limited.

I do use some of the body soaps, deodorants, and scent-killing sprays on the market, but I'm not sure that any one brand is better than another. My prehunt routine consists of showering with a scent-killing body soap, drying thoroughly with a towel, and following up with a good application of a scent-free deodorant. My clothing is washed regularly in scent-killing laundry detergent, which does a good job of not fading my hunting clothes as well as keeping them odor free. Once I get to the woods and whenever I feel the need while hunting, particularly on hot and humid days, I'll douse myself, including the area where I grip my bow, especially if it has a leather handle wrap, with a scent-killing spray. I have no proof that any of these methods actually work, but they do

Cover scents, also called masking scents, mask human scent as opposed to eliminating it. Fresh earth scent is good in any area.

boost my confidence in the woods, and that's probably the most important benefit of any of those scent-killing products, anyway.

Some hunters use cover scents, which are different from scent-eliminating formulas in that they are designed to mask or cover up human odor instead of eliminating it. The two most common cover scents are fox urine and skunk, both of which stink and neither of which will completely mask your human odor. In fact, I'd say that both odors probably make deer a little more wary instead of more at ease: A fox is a predator, and a skunk only sprays when it's alarmed or threatened.

I've also seen a product that is supposed to smell like deer dander and will reportedly make the hunter smell like another deer.

Cover scents that smell like cedar, pine, or fresh earth certainly are realistic, but they also won't completely disguise your human odor. If you do use a natural-cover scent, make sure you don't try to pass yourself off as a pine or cedar tree in an area where none is. I've often heard old-timers talk about covering their human scent by walking through fresh cow manure or rubbing strong-smelling plants all over themselves and their equipment.

I'm not passing judgment on these scent-eliminating products or techniques or anyone who uses them. What I am saying is to practice common sense when considering the use of cover scents. I don't think you can cover up or eliminate your scent to the point where white-tailed deer can't smell you, but you may be able to reduce it enough that deer won't flee immediately upon catching a whiff of you.

An incident that really showed the power and ability of the white-tailed deer's nose happened to me several years ago while on a morning hunt in one of my favorite spots. To get to my stand, I followed an old logging road through the woods, then walked off the logging road about 15 yards to the tree my stand was in. Before entering the woods, I took my usual precaution of spraying myself completely with a scent-eliminating spray. I even cleaned off the coffee I had splattered on my knee-length rubber boots. Later as I sat in my stand, I spied a young white-tailed buck walking exactly along the same path I had taken. I watched as he paused occasionally to lick the ground as though something tasty had been deposited there. He eventually ended up at the base of my tree, licking the bottom tree step. I surmised two possibilities from this behavior: either I hadn't thoroughly cleaned the coffee off of my boots, or the scent-killing spray I had used wasn't as effective as it claimed to be.

Far and away, the best way to avoid being smelled is to use the wind to your advantage. Deer can't smell you if you're upwind of them, unless the wind shifts or swirls. The weather is beyond our control, but you can study predominant wind direction in your hunting area and understand how it is affected by such factors as terrain and time of day. (For the most part, wind currents move uphill in the morning and downhill in the evening.) Whenever I approach an area I plan to still-hunt, I will ALWAYS enter from downwind, even if this means I have to get up earlier and walk farther. If you feel lazy and try to shortcut your way across the wind, you'll end up alerting every deer in the area no matter how many scent-control products you use. We'll talk more about the wind later on.

SIGHT (CAMOUFLAGE)

Camouflage is another thing I'm not sure helps hunters all that much. Oh, I still wear it, again probably just because it boosts my confidence in the woods. But according to wildlife researchers, deer can't distinguish among colors very well, so all those subtle hues and textures in the latest camouflage patterns probably don't make that much difference. What does make the difference between being seen by a deer or not is breaking up your human outline and not making any unnecessary movement. Since deer can't focus both eyes on the same object, they don't have very good depth perception, but they can spot any small movement from a long way off if they're looking your direction. If your outline is broken up, either by the pattern and silhouette of your clothing or the bush you're standing behind, chances are the deer won't know what you are. Any pattern can break up the human outline, whether it's Woolybritches Low-Visibility Camouflage, plain old plaid, or a few well-placed twigs and leaves stuck in your hat and pockets. I'm not taking anything away from the research and development folk who work for the camouflage companies, but I think they sell patterns that look better to people than deer.

An equally important part of camouflage is knowing when—and when not—to move, especially when a deer is close by.

Breaking up your outline is one of the keys to prevent yourself from being spotted by a sharp-eyed whitetail. In the top photo, I'm standing in the open, and even though I am wearing camouflage, I'm clearly visible. In the bottom photo, though, the cover makes me harder to see.

Because deer's eyes are located on the sides of their head, deer have greater peripheral vision than many animals, and this gives them the ability to see what's trying to creep up on them. In fact, they can see about 310 degrees around themselves. Deer also have excellent nocturnal vision, so be cautious on your way to the stand before daylight. Fortunately, you can fool a deer's eyes, not only by breaking up your outline but by moving very slowly when you stand a chance of being spotted. Both tactics work because deer can't focus both eyes at the same time on one object. In my early bowhunting years, I would freeze every time a deer was near. I was so afraid of being spotted that I wouldn't move, and this cost me untold shot opportunities. Eventually, I learned that you *can* get away with a certain amount of movement in the presence of white-tailed deer, as long as you take it very slow. So move cautiously, but don't turn into petrified wood every time a deer is close. The bottom line is this: If you move too much, the deer will let you know.

Native Americans often used the sun to their advantage while hunting, a tactic I have used several times myself with good results. By keeping the sun at your back and breaking up your outline, you'll make it difficult for a deer to look at you long enough to focus on what you may be. I once shot a doe with my longbow at the staggering range of 10 feet, shortly after the sun crested the horizon on a beautiful October morning. I had watched these deer for several mornings, as they crossed a wooded hilltop on their way to bed. Without much around for me to hide behind, I couldn't figure out how I was going to kill one of these deer until I remembered this old Native-American tactic. To carry out my plan, I made it a point to be in position long before daylight. Although the woods had been thinned from logging, I found a wide old ash tree to hide behind and waited for the sun to come up. Sure enough, shortly after the first rays of light spilled into the woods, the group of does crested the hill on their way to bed down for the day. As they filed past, I crouched on one knee. First one, then another

Uncovered skin is easily seen because it reflects light.

came by me, passing so close I could see every detail of their faces. Finally, the third and final doe came through. She paused, as I raised my longbow and came to full draw. But as she was staring straight into the sun at my silhouette, she failed to see the arrow as it crossed the short distance between us and buried to the fletching behind her shoulder. She died quickly, and the other two never knew what happened until I stood up.

By keeping in the shadows, you remain hidden and are less likely to be revealed by an inadvertent reflection of some shiny surface, whether it's from skin or equipment. Although I don't like to wear camouflage paint on my skin, I do wear a camouflage headnet and gloves of some type to keep the reflection of my skin to a minimum. If you don't believe that your skin reflects light, try using the palm of your hand as a "mirror" to reflect light from it onto another surface. This first came to my attention when my father told me a story about serving on a ship during World War II.

Stay far enough away from the hillcrest to avoid skylining; deer can spot this movement from a great distance.

He said that the captain of the ship instructed the members of his company not to look up while out on the deck of the ship at night, especially if they heard an airplane. The reason, he explained, is that a white face has a tendency to reflect any ambient light and could possibly give away the location of the ship by providing a target for enemy fighters.

Along the same lines, don't make the mistake of skylining yourself on the crest of a hill. When moving along high ground, stay far enough away from the hillcrest to avoid sticking out like a building on the New York skyline. Such movement is sure to attract the attention of any deer in the area, and since deer key in on movement, they will see you long before you ever see them.

You should always avoid crossing an open area, especially if you have a woodline or fencerow to use for concealment, but sometimes it's unavoidable. If you do have to cross, take a moment to make sure you're not going to bump any deer in the woods on the other side. I don't know how many times I could have avoided doing just that if I had taken a minute to scan the opposing woods with my binoculars. When crossing open areas, look for the lowest-lying area where you're sure to spend the least amount of time exposed. Keep a low profile (I'm not above low crawling, if the circumstances call for it) and move as quickly and quietly as possible to the other side. Once you get there, stop and wait for several minutes to allow normal wildlife behavior to resume.

SOUND

Make no mistake about it, deer can hear very well. Of all the sounds that we hear while in the woods, they hear even more. They must have the ability to tune it out and just listen for the important sounds.

The woods have a normal sound track similar to those relaxation tapes you can buy to help you go to sleep. The deer live in the woods and know what "normal" sounds are. Nothing can grab a deer's attention quicker than a noise that's outside of normal, especially when it's close by. I don't know how many times while stalking a deer that I've accidentally stepped on a stick. The sound of the "crack" made me cringe, as I waited for the deer's snort and white flag. But more times than not, the deer just glanced my way and went back to what it was doing. Often the deer wouldn't even look up, instead just tilting an ear in my direction as if waiting to see if the sound repeated itself. The sound of a stick breaking is a common occurrence in the woods and does not necessarily represent danger to deer. However, the *repeated* sound of sticks breaking is guaranteed to bring you under the rapid and scrupulous observation of your quarry, and any completely unnatural sounds will cause everything in the woods with ears to know precisely where and what you are. Your stealth will be irreparably damaged.

An unnatural sound can be as simple as a muffled cough, the crackling of a tiny piece of cellophane, the "tink" of an arrow against the bow riser, or even breaking wind too loudly. That's why you must ensure that every piece and part of your hunting equipment is solidly soundproofed before you ever enter the woods. Even the rubber soles of your hunting boots can produce a squeak on wet grass. I once owned a pair of high-priced, top-name hunting boots that I couldn't wear to still-hunt because every time my feet touched wet grass it sounded like someone was sliding a wet thumb across an overly inflated balloon. Needless to say, they were quickly replaced by my older, and much less expensive, knee-high rubber boots. Develop the habit of checking yourself and your equipment and fixing any sources of game-spooking noise before ever entering the woods. Make sure your bow, arrows, and quiver are noise proof, tight, and solidly mounted.

It's your mission as a traditional bowhunter to become part of the woods' natural soundtrack. Listen to the sounds other animals make as they move through the woods. You can identify most animal sounds without even seeing the animal. How many times have you heard the approach of an animal through the leaves and felt your heart beat madly for a second until you realize the animal is a squirrel and not a deer. The sound of a deer walking through leaves is magical to me. I love to hear that sound when I'm sitting in a treestand or under a tree. It has almost a swirling quality to it. The sound is so unique that it can't be mistaken for anything but what it is. The sound of a man walking through the woods is just as unmistakable. People usually move with a purpose, most often to get from point A to point B at top speed, with little regard for the sound they make. In the woods, you must learn to move silently to maintain the harmony of the natural sounds and to become part of the woods.

While still-hunting, you should always spend more time looking than moving. When you walk, take one step at a time. Place the ball of the foot lightly on the ground and feel for anything that might make noise before you put your full weight down. (Thin-soled boots or shoes will help you to feel what's under foot.) Slowly allow the back of your foot to come down as you place your full weight on that foot. Stop. Look. Listen. Feel. Once you're sure no game is around, lift your back foot and bring it forward, slowly placing the ball of the foot on the ground while maintaining your balance and keeping all of your weight on the back foot. If you feel a stick or some other obstacle underfoot, slowly move your foot to another spot. Let the ball and toes of your front foot slowly come down before bringing down the heel of that foot and shifting all of your weight onto it. Stop. Look. Listen. *Feel.* It will take some time to get used to moving in that fashion through the woods, but eventually you will "feel" the ground with your feet and won't even need to look down anymore.

Take a few minutes to unwind and get your head in the game before going hunting. You'll have much better powers of concentration.

Finally, while moving through the woods, keep in mind that a good stalker or still hunter maintains a certain mentality. If you carry a lot of "baggage" in the woods with you, it's difficult to give your full attention to what you're doing. Strange as it sounds, it's almost like the animals in the woods can feel your "bad vibes" and it makes them uneasy. That may sound like spooky conjecture on my part, but I believe that a bowhunter should have a positive mental attitude before he or she begins a still hunt. I like to sit down at the edge of the woods for a few minutes to clear my mind and get a feel for the natural rhythm of my environment. By releasing my worries or anything else that might detract from my time in the woods, I try to become a part of what's going on around me instead of a casual observer. With a little practice, you'll find that your presence will cause much less of a stir as you move along. The birds will not view you as a threat, and the squirrels will no longer bark in alarm when they see you. It's something I've never been able to fully explain, but when you get there you'll know it because you'll feel like you're finally at home.

STILL-HUNTING STRATEGIES

Because a successful hunt rarely occurs by just ambling through the woods, still hunters should never go afield without a good plan. To formulate a plan, begin by looking at the area you plan to hunt, the time of season (pre-rut, rut, or post-rut), and weather conditions, including the all-important wind direction. If you've made a map of the area, consult it before you arrive. Remember to always hunt with the wind in your favor. If it isn't possible to hunt directly into the wind and still go the direction you need to go, then move with the wind quartering to you, and always assume that everything downwind of you knows you're there. As you move slowly along, take a step or two and pause for a long, slow look in ALL directions (deer can sneak up behind you). Keep track of the wind direction by tying a 4-inch piece of floss or serving material to your bow-

A 4- to 5-inch piece of dental floss tied to the bowstring serves as an indicator of wind direction.

string, near the top string loop. If possible, pause next to some type of cover, such as a tree, a bush, or anything that will break up your outline should a deer spot you. And, always keep an eye on your back trail for any deer that may come out behind you.

I like to begin my still hunt with starting and ending points in mind. That way I can plan a route of travel that will allow me to efficiently cover the areas where I'm likely to find deer. If it's early morning or late evening, I am looking for deer on the move, and I try to hunt parallel and downwind to travel corridors and areas where deer will congregate before moving out in open fields to feed. If its midday, and not during the rut, I look for bedded deer and deer that are up and moving. By keeping in mind what the deer's activities are, depending on time of year and time of day, you'll be able to tailor your hunt to the conditions and thus increase your chances of encountering whitetails.

To give an example, I hunt a particular location on my property that does favor and rutting bucks like to cruise through during early morning. This property was logged a few years ago, and sunlight now reaches places it never did before. The resulting heavy undergrowth provides some exciting still-hunting and some occasional up-close and unexpected encounters. Since during the hunting season the prevailing wind is from the northwest, I know to approach the area and hunt it from the southeast to the northwest. The many hills and valleys on this part of the property present a real challenge when hunting on the ground. I'm lucky to make a hundred yards into the woods before mid-morning, not only because I'm moving stealthily but because I must really concentrate while hunting that type of terrain. My point is, don't go into a day of hunting with a timetable. Let the deer and your enjoyment dictate the day. Still-hunting is hard work, if you do it right, so don't feel bad about stopping for a rest from time to time. I often work up a good sweat long before the sun ever breaks the horizon.

Still-hunting is the perfect option on those really windy days when deer just aren't up and moving around like they normally are. On such days, grab your binoculars and start at the downwind side of your hunting area, picking apart every piece of cover that would likely hold a bedded whitetail. If you're patient enough, you can spy pieces and parts of the resting whitetail, just as if the animal was up and moving. The flick of an ear or tail or the movement of antlers can easily be seen from a distance if you're using good optics.

When Still-hunting Becomes Stalking

Here are a few tips for that magical moment when your still hunt becomes a stalk. Pause and take a knee next to the piece of cover you know to **always** stop next to. Watch the deer, observing its

Train yourself to always pause next to a piece of cover when still-hunting to keep from being seen in the open by deer.

body language and activity. If the animal is headed your direction or will pass by close enough for you to get a shot, don't move any further. Simply allow the deer to close the range, wait until the opportunity presents itself, and take the shot.

If the deer is moving away from you, then your job is to overtake it without getting caught. A difficult task, but possible just the same. Begin by trying to determine the deer's intended path, then pick a route for yourself that will keep you parallel and downwind of the deer. Move only when the deer's head is down, or it's looking away from you. Be patient and keep in mind that it may take several hours to catch up to the deer. Before you ever start the stalk, decide if it's worth the effort you may have to expend. Factor in the possibilities that the deer may see you and spook or a shot may never materialize. If you accidentally spook the deer, immediately freeze and watch where it goes. If not pursued, whitetails usually flee only a short distance before they stop and watch their back trail for several minutes, then resume their activity.

If you catch a whitetail bedded down, unless it's on a windy, rainy day, you have quite a chore on your hands. On a calm day, your best bet is to position yourself in front of the deer and wait for it to get up to move. But, if you're the adventurous type, try a hands-and-knees stalk. After all, that's what traditional bowhunting is all about. Just make sure you keep the wind in your face and pick out a route that will bring you within bow range before you begin the stalk. Keep a close eye on the bedded deer as you move in, and have a contingency plan in place should the deer decide to get up in the middle of your stalk. Of course if the wind is blowing a gale and it's raining cats and dog, then you can afford to be *slightly* less cautious, but you should still plan out your travel route beforehand.

Whitetails can surprise you, even during the most careful of stalks. Take these two examples that happened to me. In the first incident, I was walking along the edge of a crop field one beautiful afternoon in the middle of October. The sun was out, and I was carefully glassing the high grass at the edge of the field. As I approached a power line cut, I saw what I thought was part of a cut-down tree, lying in the tall grass not 5 feet off of the plowed field. For five minutes, I looked at this "log" through my 10x50 Bushnell's, but couldn't see any movement that would identify it as something living. I dismissed it as a log and continued working my way down the field. As I passed by this object about 15 feet away, I looked carefully again and still saw nothing to get excited about. However, after I had moved about 20 feet farther down, I heard a noise in the tall grass behind me. I turned to see the "log" had suddenly transformed into a large white-tailed doe, which stood looking at me with amusement before she bounded up the hill.

In the second chance encounter, I was hunting on a crisp, overcast morning with just a little wind, the kind of morning that is almost guaranteed to produce a parade of deer. Without warning, the wind picked up and raindrops the size of golf balls began to fall. Caught in the middle of it, I decided to hightail it to the woods, where I took cover under a downed tree with a wide trunk. As I settled under the overhanging limbs, a terrific commotion started behind me, and I shot out from under the tree at exactly the same moment a big, old white-tailed buck shot out from under the other side. We looked at each other briefly before he decided to wait the storm out somewhere else and I walked back to my truck in the pouring rain.

Such stories prove that you never know when you'll see a deer. Still-hunting and stalking deer are not for every traditional bow-hunter. Being a good still hunter requires effort, dedication, attention to detail, and pure physical stamina. But every stalk or day spent in the field still-hunting will teach you valuable lessons to make you a better hunter. And I guarantee that you will appreciate every deer you take using this ancient hunting technique.

- 5 -

Treestands
and Ground Blinds

The treestand may have done more to increase the harvest of white-tailed deer than any other invention since the firearm, but it has also contributed to more serious injuries and deaths than any other single factor in deer hunting. If you don't retain anything else you read in this book, please remember that last fact, and don't ever climb a tree or use any treestand without employing a fall-restraint system.

Having said that, today's treestands are safer and easier to use than ever before. When the first climbing stand was invented years ago, the hand climber did not exist to help in the effort. Permanent stands were usually cobbled together from scrap lumber and fastened to a tree with spike nails. Safety belts were unheard of, and anyone concerned about safety usually just tied themselves to the tree with a piece of rope.

Let's take a look at the two types of treestands, what they're meant to do, and some of the advantages and disadvantages of each type.

THE CLIMBING STAND

The earliest climbing stands were downright brutal to use. You had to hug the tree, then lift up the stand and position it using your legs and feet. By the time you reached hunting height, your arms and abdominal muscles were nearly exhausted and, depending on what type of tree you climbed, the insides of your forearms looked like raw hamburger. The stand itself was not all that sturdy once you stood on it, and a shift in your position could easily dump you out. Thanks to modern technology and computer-aided design, climbing stands today allow us to easily and safely scale trees and to remain comfortable and stable while we're up there.

Climbing stands work on the principal of tension and compression and use the hunter's body weight to lock the base of the stand against the tree and hold it there. Today's climbers are lightweight and can be set up quickly. The best models have flexible back bars, which provide more contact with the tree, and wide V-shaped channels at the base of the platform, which really grab the tree. The hand-climber section doubles as a comfortable seat, which makes it possible to sit motionless for long hours without getting fidgety. When it's time to climb down and walk out, the climbing aid straps neatly onto the platform section making a compact package. Most climbers are now made of lightweight tubular aluminum and come with backpack straps, keeping your hands free to use your binoculars or bring your stickbow into play should an unexpected shot opportunity arise.

The modern climbing stand is simple in its design. It's easy to attach to the tree, and within minutes you can climb to your desired height and be ready to hunt. Plenty of standing room on the platform section and a large, comfortable seat make it possible to shift position in mid-hunt, such as moving from sunlight to shadow, if the need arises.

The main disadvantages of a climbing stand are that it's noisy to assemble and climb with, especially before daylight, and you

Modern climbing stands, like this one by Summit, are easy to carry in and out as well as being stable and very comfortable.

must find a the tree that is reasonably straight and free of limbs on the lower trunk so that you can raise the stand to a suitable hunting height.

When selecting a climbing treestand, avoid ones that use knobs or clevis pins to secure the back bar; they're difficult to manipulate and easy to lose in the dark. Also make sure that the stand's weight limit is within a safe range and that you have read and understood all directions before attempting to use a climbing stand. Check all components before and after use, and replace any worn parts immediately. Never try to modify a climbing stand for any reason, and never attempt to climb a tree with unstable bark such as the kind found on a shagbark hickory tree.

THE LOCK-ON STAND

Fixed-position stands, also called lock-on's, are a good choice for hunters who want to leave their stand in one place. Available in both steel and aluminum with either a nylon strap or a chain-attachment system, lock-on stands also come in a range of platform sizes. For safety's sake, I recommend the widest platform you can get, especially if you hunt during cold weather and wear bigger than normal footgear. Aluminum is the best choice if you plan to leave your stand in one location for a long period of time. It can withstand long exposure to wet weather better than steel components. If you do leave your stand up year-round, conduct a safety check on it before the beginning of the season. Treestand failure due to negligence on the part of the user is a tragic yet preventable occurrence. For added safety, I normally screw a tree step into the back side of the tree, directly underneath the strap or chain. This step will serve as an emergency brake if the stand should ever slip down the tree for some reason.

Lock-on stands can be reached by tree steps that either screw in or strap to the tree or by climbing sticks, which are sections of pre-made steps that fit together and attach to the side of the tree like a ladder. Be careful when using tree steps or climbing sticks with exposed pegs; an unchecked fall from the stand can end in impalement upon one of the exposed steps or pegs. I once saw this demonstrated in graphic style on a video when a hunter dropped a trash bag filled with wet leaves from his stand. The bag caught on one of the tree steps and immediately ripped open, spilling wet leaves like entrails down the side of the tree. Very convincing, indeed! Look for tree steps and climbing sticks with enclosed pegs specifically designed to prevent this possibility. This added safety feature is well worth the small amount of extra effort and attention required to get your foot inside them.

Lock-on, or fixed-position, stands are convenient when you want to leave your stand in place year-round or when you need to hunt from a tree not suitable for a climbing stand.

Lock-on stands have advantages over climbers—they are lighter in weight and can be used in trees not suitable for climbing stands—but they do have a downside: If you decide to use your lock-on as a portable stand, you will have to carry along tree steps or climbing sticks to hang and access the stand.

SAFETY BELTS NOT AN OPTION

The first automobiles were manufactured without any sort of restraint system, even when advanced engine designs allowed vehicles to reach high speeds. The result was needless traffic fatalities. Treestands started out along this path, but thankfully hunters and treestand manufacturers had enough forethought to realize that a fall-restraint system was needed. Such a system allows hunters enough freedom of movement to draw their bows yet still provides them with a safe ending should they have the misfortune to fall from their stand. But despite this safety feature, too many hunters don't make it home at the end of the day, because far too many hunters don't wear their fall-restraint system, even though one is provided with the treestand. Chances are, if you use treestands long enough, you will suffer a fall. How you end up after the fall is completely up to you. You may think it won't happen to you, but is it really worth the risk to find out? I'm not willing to take that chance. I have a beautiful wife and five children whom I love and don't want to miss seeing grow up, so I always wear a fall-restraint system.

Several different safety systems are on the market. The earliest safety belts were just that—belts that fastened around your waist and were in turn attached to the tree. Unfortunately, what often occurred during a fall with one of these earlier models was that the safety belt would end up around the victim's chest, restricting his breathing or causing other internal injuries, or the victim would hang upside down, unable to maneuver back into an upright position. Technology and research led to the development of the full-

The full-body safety harness is the best system to arrest a fall. Most modern treestands come with one. Use it.

body harness, the safest and most effective fall-restraint method available today. The full-body harness has a strap that comes out of the harness at the top rear, right between the shoulders, and connects to another strap that is fastened, usually with a locking snap link, around the tree. Should a fall occur, the body's weight is distributed across the thighs and torso, and the body stays in an upright position, allowing the hunter to maneuver back onto the stand or at least get a hold on the tree.

Because the full-body harness is individually adjustable to every hunter, you can get a snug, comfortable fit. It can even be worn underneath heavy hunting clothes without affecting its safety or performance.

For assistance when hanging a lock-on stand, try a safety system called a lineman's belt. Used in conjunction with either climbing spurs or tree steps, the lineman's belt goes around the tree and fastens to the safety harness, freeing both hands to hang the stand and still maintain contact with the tree. The lineman's belt was once used by utility workers prior to the bucket truck and by lumberjacks of old.

The bottom line is there's no excuse for not wearing some type of fall-restraint system, especially when one is provided with the treestand at no additional cost. Wearing a safety system should be as much a part of your hunting routine as taking your bow with you to the woods. You are responsible for your own safety. Don't become a statistic!

ABOVE THE DEER

One of the main reasons so many hunters use a treestand is because it elevates them well above eye level of the deer. From their perch, they can get away with a little more movement than if they were hunting on the ground. This higher ground also may aid in keeping human scent away from the deer. How high you hunt is a matter of personal choice. I've killed deer from stands as low as 10 feet and as high as 25 or 30 feet. Your surroundings should dictate the height of your stand. If your chosen stand location has good surrounding cover and the chances of a deer spotting you are slim, then hunt lower to the ground, which will allow a flatter arrow trajectory and make it easier for you to shoot both lungs. If the area is fairly open with little undergrowth, you may need to get a little higher above the deer's line of sight. The main concerns with getting too high are that deer may spot you from a long way off and when the deer gets close enough to shoot, the increased angle of the shot may mean you'll only catch one lung instead of both. All of this, of course, hinges on having suitable trees in the area where you want to hunt.

Smart treestand hunting goes hand in hand with good scouting, something we've already covered. In particularly good locations, a lock-on stand should be hung for long-term use. I like to hang stands in areas that see high deer traffic, such as trail intersections, natural funnels, and the "hub areas" we talked about earlier. Determine where to hang a stand during your initial scouting phase when such factors as prevailing wind direction and shooting lanes can be taken into consideration. Actual hanging of a permanent stand should be done as early in the year as possible to allow any disturbance of the area to return to normal prior to the season.

Before hanging your stand, make sure it is downwind from where the deer travel, is within your effective range as a traditional bowhunter, allows you to see clearly in all directions, and is not in a tree that is going to make you stand out like a mouse in a flour sack. Try to choose a tree that provides natural cover, such as low-hanging limbs or another tree or two growing very close by. If an otherwise perfect tree has no cover to break up your outline, you might consider cutting limbs from a tree in another area and wiring or nailing them around your treestand to break up your outline. Brackets that will accept either commercially made fake tree limbs or limbs that you have taken from another tree can also be screwed directly into the tree around your lock-on stand. Such custom-made concealment won't interfere with drawing and shooting your bow. By the way, any tree limbs around your stand that interfere with safe climbing or shooting should be trimmed.

Once you've got your stand secured, take a minute to survey the immediate area, particularly any spots that might be future shooting lanes. Things look entirely different from the stand, so identify any small saplings or other obstructions that will need to be removed prior to opening day. I always carry a folding saw and roll of furnace tape with me to trim limbs and shooting lanes. By securing the folding saw to the end of a long pole with the tape, I can reach those limbs that are too high or too far away from my stand to get to. Take care of all the small details while you're there so you won't have to make another trip before you start hunting. Clean up any trimmed limbs and take them with you on the way out so that you leave the area as natural looking as possible. By the time the season rolls around, the animals will have become used to the changes in the environment, and it will be business as usual.

To make sure my permanent stands are still there when I return to hunt, I secure them to the tree. Because my lock-on stands are hung with chains, I can padlock them to prevent theft. I also clearly and permanently mark them with my name, address, and tele-phone number, just in case. Another way to deter thieves is to remove the bottom three or four tree steps or the bottom section of the climbing stick to make it more difficult to get to your stand. Whether we like it or not, thieves are everywhere. The extra few minutes you take to lock things down can prevent the scenario of arriving at your stand location on opening morning and finding the stand gone.

Finally, to complete your treestand location, don't forget to use a good bow hanger. Sitting with your bow in your lap for hours can get tiring, so it only makes sense to have something to hold it for you. Two basic types of bow hangers are available: one that screws into the tree and you actually hang the bow on to, and one that mounts on the platform of your stand and allows you to set the lower limb in a fork, with friction holding the bow in place. I prefer the hanging type that screws into the tree as it keeps the bow securely at eye level. The EZ Hanger bowholder by Realtree is the handiest bow holder made. It's articulated, which means it comes with either two or three swiveling arms that allow the hunter to place the bow in just the right position. It also has handy hooks for hanging such accessories as binoculars or rattling antlers.

TREESTAND STRATEGIES

A treestand provides the greatest possible advantage of location to help the hunter overcome some of the whitetail's legendary defenses. Because I don't like to always hunt the same area and risk contaminating a good location with too many visits, I prefer to use a climbing stand. Even my permanent stands, which I leave up year-round on a couple of my hunting properties, don't get hunted more than twice in a row. As I've said before, few forays into the whitetail woods go unnoticed. Even if you don't see any deer on a visit, they have either seen you or discovered some evidence of your passing. The more often you're there, the more scent you leave in the area and the greater the possibility of the deer changing their behavior patterns.

While in the woods scouting, I'm always on the look-out for suitable trees for locating climbing stands, depending on the wind direction during the day of a hunt. Let's say, for instance, that you have placed a stand next to a travel corridor or funnel, where the wind direction is predominantly from the north. To keep your scent from blowing to the deer, your stand should be on the south side of the area. But what if the wind happens to be blowing from the southwest on the day you want to hunt that stand location? If you have located a tree on the north side of the corridor, then place your treestand there. Climbing stands allow you to customize your hunting strategy, play the wind, and hunt from the perfect spot regardless of the restrictions our chosen hunting bows place on our shooting distance.

Although lock-on stands are designed to be put in a tree and left there, you can use them with the same kinds of portable tactics by employing just a bit more effort. As previously discussed, the easiest way to hang and access a lock-on stand is to use climbing sticks, which come in 3- to 4-foot sections and lock together to form a ladder, which is then secured to the tree by means of straps. If your primary stand is a lock-on and you decide to use climbing sticks instead of screw-in tree steps, invest in some bungee cords and fasten everything together in one neat package, which you can carry on your back to free up your hands.

GROUND BLINDS

I love to hunt deer from the ground. Nothing is as exciting as a close encounter with a deer at eye level, and a ground blind can make you just as successful hunting deer as when you hunt from a treestand. The same principles that apply to treestands—wind direction, timing, and concealment—apply to ground blinds, except that on the ground, the deer's right *there.* Sometimes you can smell them, see their eyelashes, and almost feel the steam of their breath. My heart pounds just thinking about those up-close encounters that occur in a ground blind. It's almost as good as stalking.

There are two types of ground blinds: commercially made blinds such as those produced by Double Bull and Ameristep, and blinds constructed from natural materials on hand in the hunting area itself. Either type, when properly employed, will produce results, but I really like constructing my own blind. It's satisfying and it costs me absolutely nothing except a little time and effort.

Let's talk first about constructing a ground blind from scratch. As in real estate, the key is location, location, location. Just as when

Commercially made ground blinds, such as this one by Ameristep, allow the hunter to hunt on the ground with good concealment from the sharp eyes of the whitetail.

you were searching for prime treestand locations, you want to find an area downwind (check your map for prevailing wind directions) of an established food source, travel corridor, or funnel. One of the best spots to place a ground blind is at a location, called a pinch point, where deer are forced to move through a small area, even if only for a few feet. A funnel created by two ridges, a gap in a fencerow, or the thin patch of cover connecting two blocks of woods are all good choices.

Remember that the purpose for constructing a ground blind is concealment. When you select the location, look for any naturally occurring blinds, such as downed trees, brush piles, or thickets. If nothing is available, you'll have to build your own, so find a location that won't be exposed to direct sunlight and that won't make the blind stick out like a sore thumb. Take a minute to sit down and look at the shooting areas you'll be covering. Your blind must allow you unrestricted movement when shooting, yet conceal you and your movement from the eyes of the deer. Start by marking the exact location you intend to sit, and clear out any small trees or brush that would interfere with your comfort. Mark the boundaries of your shooting lanes to make sure that you build your blind in relationship to the directions you'll need to shoot.

For building materials, use dead limbs and trees, horseweeds, tall grass, or anything else natural to the area. I recommend "importing" the material from the surrounding vicinity instead of cutting it down in the immediate area. You want your blind area to remain as natural as possible, and changing the appearance of the area around your blind (except for small changes to open up your shooting lanes) will let the deer know that something's up. Before beginning construction, lay out the dimensions of your blind, making sure to give yourself plenty of room to store your gear and whatever else you want inside the blind with you.

The best way to build your walls is first to bury dead trees or limbs (about 2 inches in diameter) vertically at 2-foot intervals along the outline of your blind. Then, weave smaller sticks and limbs between the upright limbs to form a wall. The walls can be built up as high as you like, as long as you can still shoot over them into your shooting lanes. Build the rear of the blind high enough to conceal your presence from any deer coming in from behind you, but remember to leave an opening large enough to get you and your equipment into the blind without tearing it down.

Once you've constructed the walls, use pruning sheers to trim away any sticks or limbs protruding into the inside of the blind. Next, camouflage the outside of the blind by filling in the large gaps between the sticks and limbs with tall grass, leaves, and small sticks to give it a natural appearance, much like a weathered old brush pile that's collected windblown grass, leaves, and twigs over time. Finish it off with a dead shrub or two, and you have the perfect blind. Making your own blind is a lot of work, but it also provides much satisfaction, especially whenever deer come parading by it, just like you planned. As time goes on, you can continue to import materials and build your blind up a little more. You will also have to repair any damage caused by Mother Nature or marauding livestock.

Another method of constructing your blind walls is to simply pile up dead limbs to form four walls high enough to conceal you, then trim the inside and fill in the gaps with dead leaves and such. This blind requires more trimming and is a lot less sturdy than the previously described method, but it has the advantage of being quicker to build and looking more natural.

If you find a conveniently fallen tree, depression, or other feature to conceal you from deer, use the same principles outlined in the construction tips above to turn that spot into a ground blind. Be careful when trimming any limbs from fallen trees, especially if any of the tree's weight is resting on those limbs. You don't want the fallen tree to suddenly shift position after its supporting branches are removed.

Some of my best ground blinds have consisted of nothing more than wading into a massive thicket of horseweeds and tall grass, carefully flattening out a place to sit, then cutting some small openings through the "walls" of the thicket for shooting windows. If viewed from above, this blind would stand out clearly, but from outside it's all but invisible.

So that you can hunt in different locations and different conditions, build as many of these blinds as you have the time and inclination to do.

Commercial Ground Blinds

Since the Double Bull Archery Company began marketing its ground blinds several years ago, the use and acceptance of prefabricated blinds has skyrocketed. Other companies, such as Ameristep, have started building blinds as well, providing bowhunters with numerous choices designed to work in nearly all conditions. Some of these ground blinds even come with a scent-containing liner, which claims to keep the hunter's scent inside the blind, away from the deer's nose.

Keep in mind, when choosing a ground blind, that you get what you pay for. Inexpensive ground blinds are made of cheaper materials and are less likely to withstand rough treatment or exposure to the elements. The methods used to erect the blinds differ among manufacturers; some use shock cords like a dome tent, and some use an umbrella-type opening system. Nothing can ruin a hunt quicker than struggling to put something together in the predawn darkness. Buy a blind that is well made, built to last, and user-friendly.

Also be sure that the blind you buy is big enough to allow unrestricted shooting of your longbow or recurve. Most manufactured blinds were designed for compound-bow shooters, but several models will accommodate stickbow hunters shooting the longest longbows.

By "brushing in" your ground blind, it will appear more natural, attracting less attention from a curious whitetail.

Manufactured blinds are constructed of camouflage material, but deer will still shy away from them if you don't set them up in a place that breaks up the outline of the blind. Use a few well-placed sticks and limbs to break up the obvious outline of the blind and make it blend in with its surroundings as much as possible. This tactic is known as "brushing in" by those who use these blinds regularly, and if you do it correctly, you'll notice a big difference in how close the deer will approach.

Even more important than the camouflage on the exterior is what's on the interior. The best blinds have a black liner, which won't allow light to shine through the walls of the blind and thus keeps the hunter inside from being silhouetted by bright sunlight. The liner also helps conceal any movement occurring inside the blind. The shooting windows should also be considered. Most blinds have "shoot-through" material that covers the windows, but I wouldn't trust shooting my stickbow through any kind of material, no matter how thin the material or how much the manufacturer claims the material won't affect arrow flight. A better method is to fasten strips of burlap to the inside of the blind over the windows. By parting the strips of burlap, you will maintain needed concealment but also achieve unmolested arrow flight. And finally, practice shooting from inside your blind.

When hunting from a ground blind of any type, I always take a short, sturdy, comfortable stool with me. Sitting on the ground can cause you to become wet, cold, and stiff, making it difficult to move from the ground into a solid shooting position. Whenever I go hunting, I also usually take something to drink and a high-calorie snack to keep me from getting too hungry and thirsty. Personally, I don't worry too much about scent if I need to empty my bladder, but for those of you who do, I recommend using a portable urinal with a leakproof lid. Remember, staying comfortable means you'll sit still, and sitting still translates into seeing more deer.

As you can see, there are many products to help make you a more efficient traditional bowhunter, and you can probably find something for just about every situation you're likely to encounter while hunting. Tailor your accessories to the type of hunting you do, and you'll soon notice a big difference in the number of deer you see. Just remember, your greatest opportunity for killing a deer from any treestand or ground blind location will occur during the first couple of times that you hunt it.

- 6 -

Whitetails
on Public Land

The current trend in property management is to turn large blocks of private property into hunting leases, especially in states known to produce big bucks. As a result, thousands of bowhunters have found themselves with nowhere to hunt when the prime whitetail hunting ground they've traipsed through for years suddenly becomes a private hunting club for individuals who have a lot of money to secure exclusive rights. It may not seem fair to those who are affected, but keep in mind that landowners have bills to pay just like we do.

When you consider how difficult it has become to find a piece of private property to hunt, it's no wonder more and more traditional bowhunters are turning to public land for their primary hunting grounds. Although public lands are often maligned as over-hunted, poorly managed, and a poor substitute for a good tract of private farmland, most state and federal wildlife agencies make every effort to ensure that public hunting areas provide a satisfactory experience for those who hunt there. This especially rings true in the western United States, where the sheer acreage of public land is astounding and the revenue generated by hunting is in the

More traditional bowhunters are finding the places they once had permission to hunt are now off limits. Signs like this are now appearing on more and more private property when the land is leased to clubs or individuals for a high fee.

millions of dollars. To maintain as natural a balance as possible between bucks and does and between deer and other animals, wildlife biologists keep careful track of the health and size of the deer herds on lands that they oversee.

Regardless of what you hear about public hunting land, good white-tailed deer hunting is available if you're willing to take the time and effort to locate and hunt prime areas on these tracts of land. You can put in your time and hope to get lucky, like ninety-nine percent of hunters who use public land, or you can make the commitment to aggressively find those potential hot spots that nobody else wants to go to because they're too far off the beaten path.

Public land usually falls under two categories: It is either state owned and managed or federally owned and managed. The U.S. National Park Service and the U.S. Fish and Wildlife Service, both divisions of the U.S. Department of the Interior, and the U.S. Forest Service and the U.S. Army Corps of Engineers are all actively involved in federal land management projects. Each of these agencies has a different scope of authority and different responsibilities for managing the land and enforcing game and fish regulations on those lands.

Individual states also own and manage lands that offer white-tailed deer hunting to the general public. In my home state of Indiana, the Department of Natural Resources governs all state parks and state-owned property and creates and enforces all fish and game regulations. It also sponsors special hunts inside state-owned recreation areas in hopes of reducing deer herds and lessening habitat damage caused by white-tailed deer.

The first step in hunting any of these land is to identify what public land is available to you, what its rules and regulations are concerning deer hunting (i.e., Is the deer hunting by drawing or limited access only?), and how to access the hunting areas (on foot, by horseback, etc.). Quite often, hunting on public ground means following certain rules and regulations that may not apply to private land. Some of these regulations might pertain to the use of screw-in tree steps, leaving a lock-on stand up for an extended period, or even hunting "doe only" zones.

Where you ultimately decide to hunt will depend on several factors, not the least of which is cost. Start by looking at any public hunting land close to where you live, and work your way out from there. Hunting in your own state will save you the cost of a non-resident hunting license and any other required licenses. Go to your state's home page on the Internet, and look for the web page dedicated to hunting and fishing rules and regulations. Depending on where you live and how much hunting is available in your state, you will most likely find a great deal of information here.

While researching public land in my area, I was surprised to discover that several large pieces of ground near my home were part of the Hoosier National Forest and, as such, were open to hunting. I passed this information on to a gun-hunting friend of mine, who killed a large ten-point whitetail on the property a short time later. Even though this was in the middle of Indiana's very active firearms deer season, he didn't see another hunter anywhere. This shows that research pays off. Your state, too, probably has a lot of hunting acreage that people aren't even aware of.

If you do want to make a trip to another state in hopes of bagging a trophy, start by contacting that state's Department of Natural Resources or Fish and Game Department to find out what public land is open to hunting. Also obtain information on bowhunter education and licensing requirements as well as any equipment restrictions that may apply. Remember, ignorance of the law is no excuse, so do your homework and get your questions answered before spending any money. When you make contact with the appropriate agency, also ask advice on the best places to hunt for whitetails and where you can go if you want solitude while hunting.

Regardless of where you choose to hunt, apply the same methods of scouting and planning that you use on your home turf. In chapter 3, we learned about scouting and mapping techniques and using the Internet to obtain topographical maps and satellite photos of our hunting areas. Terraserver and the U.S. Geological Survey websites will provide the necessary information you need to make an educated decision about where to hunt. By looking at a combination of a satellite photograph and a topographical map, you can obtain almost as much information about a location as if you had already been there. Detailed literature and maps of these areas are usually available from whatever agency governs hunting in your chosen state, especially if the state has multiple big-game species that generate a lot of hunting revenue.

Another good source of information is word-of-mouth. When searching for a productive hunting spot near home, talk to local fish and game officers, hikers, and maintenance personnel who spend a lot of time in and around the area where you want to hunt. Find out where they've seen deer, what times of day, how many, and what gender. Ask if any food plots are planted on the public land and whether they're legal to hunt. Find out if any wooded areas have been logged or clearcut in the last few years, providing new-growth browse for whitetails. Finally, seek suggestions on areas that are heavily hunted and should be avoided as well as out-of-the-way locations that don't see much hunting pressure.

Once you have all the information you can possibly get your hands on, it's time to put it all together in a format that will give you the big picture. Using the most detailed map that you can find, start by eliminating land that you can't hunt. Most public hunting land will have restricted areas, and most states prohibit hunting within a certain distance of a roadway. Using a pencil, lightly mark those areas off the map. Next, eliminate all ground within a half mile of any parking areas or ATV or hiking trails. What you have remaining is ground that isn't easily accessible by either vehicle or foot traffic but is a magnet for white-tailed deer, which naturally seek areas where they're not likely to be disturbed. If you received any tips or secondhand information on good hunting spots, plug those into your map and see if they correspond with any locations that you've already identified as possibilities.

Now, you just need to get out and burn a little boot leather by exploring and scouting your future hunting areas to see if things look as good in real time as they did on your maps and satellite photographs. Typically, I don't like to spend much time in areas I plan to hunt, but since this is public ground, you're not going to have any control over who wanders through the area anyway. By already eliminating ground with little or no potential, you've already saved yourself a lot of walking. Look for out-of-the-way food sources, such as oak ridges where deer can feed without being bothered by hikers or ATV riders. Also try to identify bedding locations far from any traveled or easily accessible areas. The same deer hunting principles apply on public ground as they do on private property. The only difference is that public land has a greater number of hunters, and this makes the deer a lot less tolerant of human presence. There's no way around it—the farther you get from easily accessed areas, the better your chances of finding deer.

Before you hunt a new area, make sure you're perfectly clear on the boundaries of the hunting areas and public property. Several areas on one of my favorite pieces of public land butt right up against private property, and the only way I know exactly where the private property starts is a single strand of wire stung through some trees with rusty old "Private Property" signs every hundred yards or so. Be aware that there may be places where no obvious line exists between public and private property. No piece of hunting real estate, regardless of how good it is, is ever worth being prosecuted for trespassing.

As you're scouting, pay particular attention to any firebreaks or fire trails, which are gaps in the trees and underbrush designed to contain the fire to a certain area and thus limit damage from forest fires. If these trails are accessible to vehicular traffic, you'll see tire tracks. But you can also use these dirt roads to identify trail crossings by locating and following deer tracks where they enter and leave the fire lane. One year, I unintentionally came across a deer-hunting hot spot using this method and ended up taking a nice buck with my stickbow. I had followed a set of large deer tracks along the fire lane before they returned to the woods. Because the ground in the woods was soft enough, I was able to follow these tracks for nearly a mile, until they led to a heavily traveled deer trail that ran perpendicular to a river and eventually intersected with another deer trail, which ran alongside the river down to a crop field. The crop field itself was on private property, but the deer would travel back into the woods after feeding in the crop fields at night. Several weeks later, I returned to the spot with a climbing stand on my back and was rewarded with shooting what was the largest buck of my career at the time. I was far enough back in the woods that I never saw a sign of another human being, and to this day it remains one of my favorite hunting spots.

When hunting on public land, be prepared to stay on your stand longer than normal. In heavily hunted areas, whitetails become accustomed to the comings and goings of other hunters and will adjust their behavior accordingly. Since most deer hunters will leave the woods around nine or ten o'clock in the morning, depending on the weather and the deer activity, and will usually return a couple of hours before dark, the deer begin to move in the middle of the day to avoid contact. Often when hunting public property, I'll sleep in and won't even head for the woods until ten or eleven o'clock. I'll still-hunt back to my area and hunt during the middle of the day, often seeing more deer and fewer hunters than I would have earlier or later in the day. If you find an area that looks like it should hold deer, yet you aren't seeing them early or late, try hunting the middle of the day. You may be quite surprised by what you discover.

Also remember that the deer you hunt on public land, even if you searched out the most remote locations, have been subjected to heavy hunting pressure and therefore will exhibit behavior unlike what you would expect from less-pressured whitetails on private property. Bucks on public land may not exhibit any appreciable rubbing or scraping activity, and they may not respond well to rattling or grunting because they've heard and seen it all before. Any calling should be sporadic and low in volume, and if you must rattle, try to imitate a short, non-aggressive sparring match between two smaller bucks by gently meshing the tines and "tickling" the tips together. Decoys work well on public land as they help to reinforce a deer's sense of safety by making it believe another deer is in the area. A well-placed decoy, coupled with judicious use of a nondominant urine scent, can help draw an otherwise unsocial deer into stickbow range. Collapsible decoys, such as those made by Renzo's or Jerry McPherson's Montana, work well. They're easily transportable and completely concealable, making you much safer walking with one to and from your stand. If you do carry a full-body decoy into the woods, whether it's on public or private property, remember to always cover the lifesize decoy completely with a hunter orange tarp or piece of cloth to avoid a senseless accident.

The best time to hunt public land is from opening day of bow season to the beginning of any firearms season, since fewer bowhunters make for a lot less competition for hunting turf. Even though the rut coincides with the beginning of the firearms season in many states, it's been my experience that bowhunting on public property at this time is somewhat like trying to thread your way through a live-fire range, especially if the area holds a good population of whitetails. The deer are generally in a panic, and if you do get a shot, it'll probably be at a gray streak as the deer heads for safer territory.

Still-hunting is not a good idea during the firearms season, unless you're absolutely *positive* that the area you plan to still-hunt has a low number of hunters and you're well covered with hunter orange. Even then, you're unlikely to encounter many deer that aren't extremely alert to their surroundings. You're much better off sticking to one small area and letting the gun hunters push deer past you.

Late-season hunting on public ground can be productive as long as the firearms season has closed and the woods have gone back to normal. After the rut, and when the weather turns foul, usually only diehard bowhunters will endure the elements for a chance to put more meat in the freezer. The deer are keying in on food sources at this time. The bucks need to eat to get their strength back up after the rut, and does are trying to store body fat so they'll give birth to healthy fawns the following summer. Here's where your scouting comes into play as you have already identified secondary food sources far from the areas most frequently used by people. Because acorns provide the highest fat content, deer will consume them by the bushels wherever they can still be found. A good way to locate oak groves at this time of year is to search for feeding squirrels that are busy getting ready for the winter.

DON'T GET LOST!

Before hunting on public land, or anywhere for that matter, make sure someone knows where you will be going and what time to expect you back. Always carry an emergency survival kit, containing at the minimum a space blanket, waterproof matches, a compact flashlight, and a loud whistle.

When hunting unfamiliar property and large tracts of public land, it's quite easy to get turned around, even for those with impeccable woodsmanship skills. The vast majority of public land open to hunting is unimproved, and if you don't pay attention to landmarks or use a trustworthy method of tracking where you are, you can get into some serious trouble long before you even realize you're lost.

Picture this. You're hunting on a large piece of public hunting ground, when on a distant ridge, you spot a monster white-tailed buck chasing a doe. You watch them for several minutes, and then when the deer go down the other side of the ridge, you take off after them in the hopes of getting a shot at that big buck while he's occupied. You crest the ridge quietly, only to see them working their way across the next ridge, about 200 yards over. Not willing to give up, you follow. When you get there, you find two sets of tracks leading down into a valley. Heart pounding with excitement, you follow slowly, keeping your eyes on the ground ahead, not paying any attention to landmarks or which direction you're headed. Sud-

A quality compass or GPS unit can bring you home safely at the end of a long day in unfamiliar terrain.

denly the tracks disappear, and you have no idea which way the deer went. With growing alarm, you also realize that you have no idea where *you are.* What now?

What has been in use by the U.S. military for years has recently become affordable for everyone, opening up a whole new method of land navigation. GPS systems have taken the place of the good old map and compass. GPS, which stands for Global Positioning System, works by using numerous satellites in the earth's orbit to determine your exact location by latitude and longitude on the ground. Depending on how advanced your GPS unit is and how many satellites it can pick up at a particular time, you can find out your location to within plus or minus 3 feet. These units also give you the ability to record your location at different points as you go along, and by following these waypoints in reverse, you can back out of an area exactly the same way you went in. You can also record locations where you would like to come back later to hunt, either by entering a name or title for a particular waypoint, or by recording the location's latitude and longitude in a log book. Then when you plug the coordinates into the GPS system, you will be led right back to the exact location you wanted to hunt. As a side-note, the Terraserver website also provides the exact latitude and longitude for the area on a satellite photograph. So if you happen to be "Internet scouting" and decide to hunt an area, all you have to do upon your arrival is plug the coordinates into your GPS unit and it will lead you to the same spot you looked at in the satellite photograph. By the same token, you can record the latitude and longitude of any spot in the woods on your GPS system, so that later you can locate that spot in a satellite photograph on the Internet. How's that for helpful?

When choosing a GPS system, get one that's *weatherproof,* rather than weather *resistant.* Garmin and Magellan are the top two manufacturers of civilian GPS systems, and they have several outstanding features, including built-in barometers and compasses and the ability to interface with a computer to download maps of certain areas. Some units even have the capacity to operate as walkie-talkies with a fairly decent range. A good GPS unit should be able to withstand rough handling and still function without fail. If you're going to place your full confidence in the unit, spare no expense and make sure you carry plenty of spare batteries. Before relying solely on GPS to navigate through large blocks of unfamiliar ground, make sure you understand how to use and operate the unit. Also, either carry a spare GPS unit as a backup or learn to navigate by the most trustworthy and time-proven method there—the map and compass.

For those of you who are old-fashioned like me and either don't want to spend a lot of money on GPS or don't want to rely on something electronic, a map and compass will still serve you well. While an infantry soldier in the Army, I became well versed in map reading and land navigation, a skill I still rely on on a regular basis. But, you don't have to be a veteran of the armed services to learn land navigation. With a topographical map and a quality compass, anyone can navigate from point A to point B quickly and accurately. As a matter of fact, if you know your location on a good topographical map, you can navigate from one location to another by matching up terrain features on the map with the actual corresponding terrain features that you see on the ground. That's how accurate topographical maps are. Land navigation by terrain association is somewhat advanced and should never be attempted by anyone who is not well versed in the practice, but in an emergency it's important to know how to do it accurately. You should always carry a quality compass with you when you're in the woods and before entering the woods, take a compass reading so you'll at least know the general direction you'll be traveling. It is quite possible to get turned around, even in woods you're familiar with, and that simple piece of equipment is enough to get you home. Know how to use it.

Learning how to use a map and compass or a GPS unit is simple, and you can find many books on the subjects at your local public library. I strongly urge anyone who wants to hunt on public land of any size to learn land navigation to avoid the embarrassment and danger of becoming lost.

If You Do Get Lost . . .
Don't panic! Once you realize you're lost, stop where you are. The biggest mistake people make when they get lost is to try to find their way back. You should have told someone where you are, what time you'll be back, and when they need to push the panic button, so by moving around you'll only frustrate the efforts of rescuers to locate you. If you're carrying your cell phone and have a signal, contact authorities and notify them of your general location.

If you have no method of contacting anyone, seek the closest sheltered area you can. Every ten minutes or so, blow your emergency whistle in three series of three short blasts, which is Morse code for an emergency. If you have to stay in the woods overnight, build a small fire and use your space blanket to maintain your body heat.

If you have any concerns about becoming lost for a long period of time, educate yourself on survival skills by reading as much material about the subject as possible and put together a survival kit that will fit in a daypack or fanny pack.

GETTING DEER OUT OF THE "BACK 40"

When hunting public property, it's a known fact that the farther you move away from roads and traveled areas, the better the hunting, but this also means that when you're successful in your hunt, you have a job on your hands getting the deer out of the woods. I don't believe in ATV use on public hunting land, but I recognize that it may be necessary, where legal, to use a vehicle to get your deer out of the woods to prevent ruining the meat. In states where it's allowed, you can quarter the animal or bone out the meat, making it possible to pack the animal out on your back. In Indiana and probably other states as well, the deer may be field dressed but must remain whole with the head and hide still attached until the animal is checked in at a registered deer-check station.

Keeping the animal whole can present quite a problem, especially if you have a long way to transport it. I once killed a large buck on public land in a location far from where I parked my truck. Fortunately, I had a hunting partner that day, and we managed to drag the deer the entire distance back to the truck. By the time we reached the truck several hours later, the entire side of the deer was hairless, ruining the cape. I suppose we could have tied the deer's legs together and carried it on a pole, but the deer weighed well over 200 pounds field dressed so that probably wouldn't have been any easier.

Don't limit the size of your hunting area by how far you can drag a deer. Shortly after the deer-dragging marathon I mentioned above, I purchased a deer cart, and this allows me to expand my range on public property, and makes me more self-sufficient while hunting alone.

Deer carts are indispensable, and there are many different styles and models in all price ranges to choose from. The most important feature for a user-friendly cart is the size and angle of the tires. Tubeless solid tires are a better option than bicycle-type tires, since you won't have to carry spare inner tubes and inflation devices. The wider the tires and the larger their diameter, the easier they are to pull and the better they resist sinking into mud. The wheels on my deer cart are actually angled, which makes it easier to pull the cart across rough terrain and soft ground. The wheels should spin on heavy-duty closed bearings that keep dirt and other debris from affecting smooth operation.

Portability should also be considered when deciding on a deer cart. Carts that disassemble easily or have folding handles are easier to transport and assemble prior to use, which is especially helpful when the bed of the truck also has to carry one or two large coolers, hunting equipment, and a couple of deer to boot.

Don't forget about straps to secure your deer onto the cart. I like to use ratchet straps and rubber bungee cords to keep the deer from moving around or falling off during transport. Loading the deer belly-up on the cart, with the head near the handle, protects the animal's horns and keeps the head from interfering with the wheels. I fold the deer's legs down against its body and secure them with bungee cords and then cover the entire animal with a hunter orange cloth or tarp to keep it clean during transport and to identify myself to other hunters.

SUCCESSFUL HUNTING

The keys to successfully hunting public land can be summed up quite simply.

1. Contact the proper state or federal agency to find out what property is available to hunt.

A deer cart makes it possible to get animals out of just about anywhere. The angled tires keep the cart from sinking too deep in soft soil.

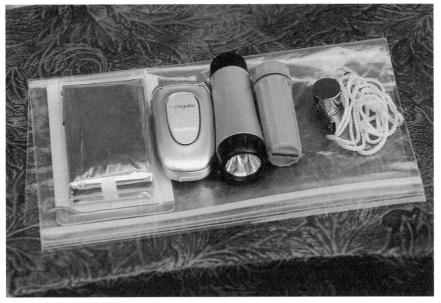

Never go hunting without at least a space blanket, cell phone, small flashlight, matches in a waterproof container, and loud whistle.

2. Determine what licenses/permits are required when hunting out of state.
3. Research the area as thoroughly as possible, using topographical maps and satellite photos. Identify possible hunting locations with your "long-distance scouting techniques," and mark them on your maps and photos. Make sure you're familiar with all boundaries.
4. Eliminate areas that are off-limits, receive high traffic, or are otherwise unproductive, and show these places on your maps and photos.
5. When possible, travel to the location before hunting season and scout the areas you hope to hunt.
6. **Before you go hunting, make sure someone knows where you are and when to expect you back.** Go as far as filing a written plan with someone, letting them know when you're

back home safely, and advising them to contact authorities if you're not back by a certain time and date.

7. Always carry an emergency survival kit with you, no matter how simple it is. Also, carry a cell phone whenever possible.

With a little planning and forethought, hunting on public property can be a highly successful venture. The deer are there, they're just harder to hunt than their counterparts who live relatively unmolested lives on private property and may never have felt the pressure of being hunted. Scores of whitetails, including many trophy bucks, are harvested on public land every year. By doing your homework and hunting harder and smarter than other hunters, you'll be a successful traditional bowhunter. Just make sure you hunt safely, follow all the rules and regulations, and leave the land just as you found it.

- 7 -

Hunting the Rut and Using Calling, Rattling, and Scents

The rut is to whitetail hunting what the Daytona 500 is to stock-car racing. It's the time of year when traditional bowhunters stand the best chance of arrowing a big buck. Weather conditions are suitable for deer movement all day long, and it pays to stay in the stand from sunup to sundown.

Every deer hunter has an idea of when the rut starts in a particular area, but what really begins the rut is the first doe to come into estrous. Bucks also recognize the time of the year and become a lot less tolerant of each other's presence. The bachelor groups you've been watching all summer will have dissolved as pushing and shoving turns to real fighting in an effort to establish dominance for breeding rights among bucks of relatively equal physical stature.

What brings does into estrous and causes this behavioral change in bucks? Scientists tell us it's photoperiodism, which is a chemical change that occurs in the animal's pineal gland due to the gradual shortening of the length of the days. Scientists even say it's possible to cause a doe to come into estrous at any time of the year by keeping her inside a windowless room and gradually shortening the amount of light she is exposed to each day. This method supposedly is used by many of the companies that need to produce a marketable quantity of doe-in-heat urine lures in time for the season.

Unfortunately, it's difficult to predict the exact dates of the whitetail rut with any degree of accuracy. Some believe that the rut occurs around the second full moon following the fall equinox. Others believe that it's triggered by a lengthy stretch of cool weather. I believe that colder weather does have something to do with it when you look at the way the rut occurs from north to south in the continental United States. Deer on the U.S.-Canadian border come into estrous before the does in Texas do. In Indiana, the rut usually lasts for about two weeks in early November, while the rut in Texas might start in late December and run all the way into January.

Although the rut still contains many mysteries not understood by biologists, certain predictable behaviors are exhibited by both bucks and does. We know that white-tailed bucks will chase does before they come into estrous, and that once a buck finds a receptive doe, he'll stay with her and breed her several times before resuming his search for estrous does. It was previously thought that a single buck would remain with an estrous doe and be the only one to breed her when she's in season, but now biologists believe that some white-tailed does actually breed with more than one buck. Timing is crucial since not every doe will come into estrous at the same time and the actual length of time a doe is in heat is very short. Any doe that is not successfully bred during the initial rut will come into estrous again twenty-eight days later. When you see bucks trailing does hot and heavy and behaving like village idiots, you know the rut is in full swing.

These facts may not put us in the right place at the right time to intercept a buck on the hunt for an estrous doe, but we can use this information to shade the odds in our favor, beginning with hunting where the does hang out. You already know these locations if you've done your scouting correctly, and you should have a rut hunting location picked out. Remember, a white-tailed buck may travel several miles in search of estrous does, but a white-tailed doe moves only in search of food and will stay inside her home range almost exclusively.

The real key to whitetail hunting success during the rut is to spend as much time as possible in the woods, hunting the prime areas. If you have got a week of vacation you don't know what to do with, now's the time to burn it. This is the time of the year to pull out all the stops. Early in the season, I like to hunt the fringes of cover and the outskirts of food sources, simply to avoid letting the deer know they're being hunted. I'm saving everything for the rut. Now is when I begin hunting aggressively because *all* of the deer will be moving more than ever before. Not only is the cooler weather more comfortable for them, but every buck in the woods has his nose in the rump of every doe he comes across.

Be prepared to stay on your stand, in your blind, or in the woods from daylight to dark during the rut. Although whitetail movement during the early season is best at dawn and dusk, you never know when you'll encounter deer during this time of year. I've watched bucks that I've never seen before wander past my stand or blind in the middle of the day, nose to the ground in search of a hot doe. Be prepared for a long day: Take high-calorie snacks and water with you, and dress according to the weather. Some hunters even take "relief bottles" with them to their stand, a good idea if you drink a lot of water or had a lot of coffee before heading out to hunt. Your comfort will allow you to concentrate on what's going on around you and will make the day much more enjoyable.

USING SCENTS

There are three basic categories of deer attractant scents. Food scents appeal to a deer's sense of hunger and work all season long.

Sex scents appeal to a deer's need to procreate and, depending on the strength and chemical formula, can be used before, during, and after the rut. Curiosity scents arouse a deer's curiosity but not necessarily the hunger or sex drives and can be effective any time.

Every scent or lure on the market claims to be the best at what it does, and we've all seen the advertisements showing proud hunters and their behemoth bucks with the caption underneath: "Without Brand X doe-in-heat lure, I never would have killed this beauty!" Well, that may or may not be. But a lot of other factors besides Brand X made that hunter successful. More often than not, he was in the right place at the right time and made a good shot under pressure. I think occasionally these deer attractants lure hunters much better than they lure deer, but I'm also sure that some of them work under the right conditions. Each type of attractant has a correct method of application, and we'll talk about these next.

Food Scents

Food scents, which appeal to a deer's hunger drive, should not be confused with baiting. Baiting is the use of an actual food product, whether it's carrots, apples, or sugar beets, to attract deer to a specific area. Deer follow the tempting odor to its source and actually will have something to consume once they find it. Baiting is legal in some states but not in others. No offense to those who hunt deer over bait piles—I've heard the stories of hunting pressure being so heavy in an area that hunters do everything they can to get a deer close enough to shoot—but I don't think baiting is necessary if you take the time to find the right spot to hunt.

Food scents, on the other hand, tickle the deer's nose with the smell of some tasty snack and encourage the deer to seek the source of the odor. When the deer shows up, it finds no bait pile or food source, only a hunter patiently waiting for the deer to arrive. Food attractant scents include acorn, apple persimmon, sweet corn, molasses, and even peanut butter.

Food scents, such as these acorn-scented solid wafers, appeal to hungry deer.

These scents can be used near your ground blind or treestand as a way to stop and hold a deer long enough to provide a shot. Simply apply the scent to a bush, shrub, or the side of a tree (about 3 feet off the ground to get the scent dispersed) in a location where you have a good shot. A word of caution: Food scents may appeal to a deer once or twice, but as soon as it figures out that there's really nothing to eat the deer will lose interest quickly. Also, don't think for a minute that these scents will draw deer from a long distance; they're just not that effective.

No discussion of food lures would be complete without talking about mineral-based deer attractants. Although illegal to use for hunting purposes in Indiana, mineral products that can be either mixed with water and poured on the ground or placed directly on the ground and allowed to leech into the soil *will* draw deer from long distances. Mineral attractants come in liquid form to be poured over rotting tree stumps, inducing the deer to lick and chew the rotting wood to get the tasty minerals out of it, or in sold form with simple blocks flavored with everything from persimmon to sweet corn. If you plan to use these products, which are basically a form of baiting, make perfectly sure it is legal to do so in your state.

Sex Scents

The most useful of the three types of scents, sex scents are available in the widest variety and can have the most dramatic effect when used correctly. They are intended mainly to attract white-tailed bucks, but does will also come to find out who the new deer are in the neighborhood.

Sex scents can be in the form of doe-in-heat urine, which is designed to sexually arouse any bucks that catch a whiff; "dominant buck" urine, which is intended to cause dominant bucks in the area to go into a fit of rage; or tarsal gland lure, which is supposed to fool big bucks into believing that another buck is in the area

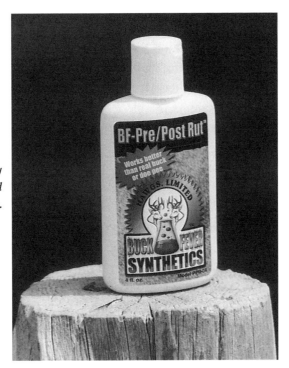

Sex scents mostly consist of deer urine and attract bucks and does.

competing for does. (Dominant buck and doe-in-heat urine are most effective right before and during the rut. Use them any other time, and you'll likely scare off deer instead of attracting them.)

Although not actual sex scents, forehead gland scent provides the odor left behind when bucks rub their antlers on a tree or licking branch, and interdigital gland scent is the odor left behind by the gland between a deer's hooves. With a combination of these different scents, a good stickbow hunter can set up his or her own little whitetail soap opera by fooling deer in the area into believing that a whole slew of activity is going on that they're not privy to.

I like to set the stage for my little soap opera at the beginning of deer season by leaving forehead gland lure on a couple of low-hanging branches in the area of my treestands and ground blinds. Then, I'll create a few mock scrapes under low-hanging branches in the shooting lanes of my stands and blinds, and add about an ounce of urine on the ground and a squirt of forehead gland lure on the overhanging branches. Just use plain doe urine at this time, because the does aren't in estrous yet and bucks know it. I use the synthetic lures made by Hawgs Limited for a couple of reasons. First, being synthetic they have an indefinite shelf life. Second, they contain solids that will stay on the ground for a longer period of time than real urine, and any moisture, such as a shower or dew, will reactivate the odor, almost like the scent has been redeposited. Hawgs Limited offers three different scents: a pre/post-rut urine lure, which has a milder odor and will work any time of the year; a rut lure, which is much stronger and works on both does and bucks during the rut; and a forehead gland lure, which helps to "dress up" your mock scrapes and make them more authentic.

As the rut approaches, I'll apply a healthy dose of the rut formula to my mock scrapes, and I'll twist and break the ends of the licking branches above the scrape to make them look like they've been worked over by a frustrated buck. Another squirt or two of forehead gland lure on the licking branch and I'm almost done. At a couple of spots around the perimeter of the scrape, I'll squirt some pre/post-rut lure and throw in a little (just a little, mind you) interdigital gland or tarsal gland lure to make it appear as though several deer of both sexes were in the area. Since I don't hunt any stand more than twice in a row without giving it a break for several days, I'll freshen all my scents each time I return to hunt. As time goes on, I'll begin to notice different deer tracks in my scrapes, and as the rut approaches, I'll usually come in one day to find that my scrapes have been demolished and new ones established nearby. I've had excellent success with this ruse on many different occasions, and at least one nice buck shows up sometime when I'm on stand. I don't always get them, but their appearance is frequent enough to make me believe that my setup is working. A word of caution, in case you decide to try this for yourself: Always make sure that you're as scent free as possible when setting up your scrapes, and wear rubber gloves any time you have to touch something that you can deposit your scent on.

Sex scents are also effective when used on drag rags to create trails to and around your stand. Be realistic, and instead of trying to create a scent trail a mile long, make one about 100 to 150 feet. Don't worry about freshening your drag rag as you go along. When a white-tailed deer urinates on its tarsal glands or steps in urine, it doesn't stop every so often to refresh the scent. The scent will gradually diminish with distance, and that's how a deer knows what direction the other deer was traveling. To create your trail, lay the drag rag on the ground, saturate it with scent, and begin walking toward your stand, but continuing past the stand instead of walking to it. Remember, you want the deer out from your stand where you can shoot it, not right underneath you. You can also hang the drag rag in a nearby bush like a scent wick as a means of stopping the deer for a shot.

While we're on the subject, scent wicks are another good method of dispersing your favorite scent. Simply saturate several wicks and hang them in a half circle on the downwind side of your hunting spot, making sure that each one is hung in a spot that you can shoot at. If your luck is like mine, the deer inevitably will nose up to the scent wick that I hung behind a bush.

Scent bombs work along the same lines as wicks, except they actually contain more scent and won't evaporate or dry out as quickly. You can buy bombs with screw-on lids or make your own using empty 35-millimeter film canisters and cotton balls. Just saturate the cotton with your favorite lure and use them like a scent wick. When you're done hunting, replace the caps and store them for next time. I tape a pinch-type clothespin to the side of the canister so I can hang it from a tree limb or bush. Like any method of scent dispersal, they work best when placed about 3 feet off the ground so the wind can carry the scent down range.

Scent bombs (top) and wicks are excellent methods of dispersing deer lure, as well as stopping deer in a specific spot for a standing shot.

Sex scents have become more popular as manufacturers develop different twists on the old originals. Once only available in liquid form, they now have been developed into paste or gel forms that will remain potent for a much longer period of time than liquids. You can also find scents in a powder or crystal form, which "renews" itself whenever moisture comes in contact with it. These work well for mock scrapes, since you won't have to refreshen the scent as often.

Curiosity Scents

Curiosity scents fall into a category somewhere between sex lures and food scents and are often a combination of both. The most common curiosity scent on the market is Wildlife Research Center's Trail's End #307. With either vanilla or anise as a base, these scents work any time of year by appealing to the deer's sense of curiosity. Just as we walk into a candle or coffee shop to enjoy the smell, deer often investigate these lures because they smell good. The lure doesn't even have to smell good, as I've had old-timers tell me that one of their favorite deer lures was beaver castor. These elderly gentlemen explain that applying a dab of castor to the downwind side of a tree will draw in any buck from miles around. I wouldn't have believed it had they not produced weathered old photographs showing big bucks, the likes of which we don't see too often anymore.

Probably the best way to use curiosity lures is to apply them to a boot pad or a drag rag and walk a pattern leading to your treestand or ground blind. Then hang the boot pad or drag rag in a spot that will provide a good shot at any deer that stops to investigate. Curiosity lures can work on deer of either sex, so you're as likely to see a big doe following your scent trail as you are a buck.

Under the right conditions, attractant scents have the potential to bring deer into your area and hold them there long enough for you to get a shot with your trusty traditional bow, but they are not

Curiosity scents, often a combination of sex and food scents, are effective all season.

a substitute for good scouting, stand or blind placement, or shooting skills. On a final note, attractant scents have no application when you're still-hunting. Never apply a deer lure to yourself, your clothing, or your equipment because you don't want the deer looking for YOU. You also don't want to risk being attacked by a white-tailed buck by applying certain types of lures to your clothing. Although not common, such attacks have been documented, some of which have resulted in serious bodily injury. I know of the story of one unfortunate soul who didn't even purposely apply the lure to himself, but the bottle accidentally leaked into the cargo pocket of his hunting pants. Instead of a white-tailed buck, it was a black angus bull that came after him. I was that unfortunate person, and although I'm not sure if the leaked doe-in-heat lure aggravated the bull or not, I do know that I had walked by him a hundred times in the past and he never acted like that before!

RATTLING AND CALLING

Deer calling, when used in conjunction with attractant scents, presents a more realistic scenario to any incoming deer, and although the most common goal, it is not limited to calling only bucks.

I love to rattle, and I've had good success with it on a few occasions. But experts say, and I have to agree, that just because you smack a set of antlers together doesn't mean every white-tailed buck in the woods is going to throw caution to the wind and come charging in looking for a fight.

Many factors determine a buck's response to your rattling, with the biggest being the buck-to-doe ratio in your particular hunting area. If does are around every corner, but few mature bucks can be found, there's not much competition for breeding. Rattling in this scenario is not going to bring the response you see on your favorite television hunting show. White-tailed bucks are individuals, just like traditional bowhunters. Some don't mind confrontation and actually enjoy a good scuffle. Others are shy and retiring, preferring to live a quiet life and settling for the occasional receptive doe instead of trying to breed everything on four legs.

During the pre-rut, bucks spar to establish a pecking order. The spars are playful at first, but as the hormones start flowing and the rut gets closer, these jousting matches can get quite rough, even to the point of causing significant injury or death to the loser. By the time the rut arrives, the hierarchy within a local breed has pretty much been established until bucks outside the area start drifting in looking for does to breed.

Rattling attracts bucks for a couple of reasons. Smaller bucks respond out of curiosity to see what's happening, much like kids on a playground will crowd around a fight. They don't have much desire to participate, though. Mature bucks respond to see who's fighting and to look for a receptive doe that he can cut off from the others and breed himself. Or maybe he shows up to settle any question about who is the toughest buck in the woods.

What you rattle with should sound realistic. I've used real antlers and rattling bags successfully. When using real antlers, the antlers should be roughly the same size of the bucks in your hunting area. In other words, if you only have 120-class bucks in your area, don't rattle with 150-class antlers and expect a response. As a matter of fact, some of the best results may occur with very small antlers. A friend of mine used a set of fork horn antlers to rattle in and kill a 160-class white-tailed buck with his bow. This buck was being followed at a short distance by a 130-class deer.

When rattling first became popular, hunters believed that by really grinding and cracking the antlers together, they would get a more rapid response. Since then, it has been decided that merely tickling the antler tips together and gently meshing the tines is safer and may evoke more responses. Once again, it just depends on the mood and attitude of any buck that may hear your rattling. If he's aggressive, he may come charging right in looking for a fight. But more likely, he'll circle around downwind and come in

Real antlers (shown), fake antlers, or rattling bags can all work if used correctly.

silently to confirm with his eyes what his ears are hearing. Your attractant scents will pay off now, especially if he gets a whiff of what he thinks is another buck. Decoys, especially the full-body models with detachable legs and antlers, also make for an exciting hunt. Deer normally approach a decoy from the front to make sure that this "deer" sees them coming. For that reason, always place your decoy facing to your right or left and slightly toward you. And don't forget to drape a hunter orange cloth or tarp over your decoy when you're carrying it in or out of the woods.

When watching the hunting shows we all love, keep in mind that for all the successful rattling scenes you see, a lot more unsuccessful tries become useless footage on the cutting-room floor. Unless you live in a whitetailed battle zone, you simply will not hear the constant crashing of antlers in the woods, even in the heat of the rut. Use rattling sparingly and tailor your methods to the response you get. If you sit and bang horns together all day, bucks are going to know something isn't right. Rattle for two or three minutes intermittently, then set the antlers down for a couple of hours. A response may take some time, but while you're watching, keep your eyes peeled for that buck trying to sneak in on the downwind side of you.

Deer calling and the calls themselves have made great strides in their effectiveness over the last few years as whitetail biologists and deer call manufacturers have come to better understand the vocalizations of white-tailed deer. All the same, some calls border on the ridiculous and are designed to take your money instead of calling in deer. I'll say this: Beware of fads and the "latest and greatest" calls on the market. They come out every year, even from the better names in the business.

The main vocalizations that traditional bowhunters should know are the doe bleat and the buck grunt. I don't pretend to understand the whitetail's language, and I often wonder if anyone really does. I have one deer call, and it makes every whitetail vocal-

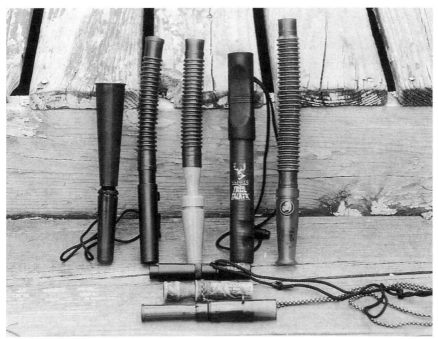

Many calls on the market reproduce the vocalizations of white-tailed deer, from grunts to bleats, but I favor the True Talker. By pressing down on different spots on the call, you can make many different sounds.

ization I need. By pressing on the barrel of the call, I can make either a grunt from a young or mature buck or a doe bleat. These are the only vocalizations I use.

I use the doe bleat to try and fool deer into believing that a doe is in the area. If I see a doe, especially during the rut, I will bleat to her in an effort to bring her in and hold her in the area so that she may lure in a buck. Quite often, I'll end up taking her home in the bed of my truck, as most of my hunting areas have a high doe population. The vocalization I use is a short (about one and a half seconds long) bleat, what is often referred to as a contact bleat. It's my way of saying, "Hi, I'm over here. Come join me." I have no idea what I'm really saying, but it seems to work and that's all I need to know.

Buck grunts are a different story. If I see a buck or bucks, I'll give a couple of short (about a second long) grunts to get their attention. If the buck has any interest in what I'm saying, I'll know right away. He'll either start my way—then I'll stop using the call and let him approach—or he'll stand there, start milling around, or begin walking off—in that case, I'll grunt louder, continuing until the buck looks my direction. Once I'm sure he's heard me, I'll stop grunting. At this point, the buck will either come in or he won't, and I don't think there's anything you can do to convince him otherwise.

I also grunt when I'm rattling. This is just an occasional short, loud grunt to make it sound like I'm a buck putting forth a little effort in a shoving match and I want the other buck to know I mean business. I don't grunt constantly during the rattling sequence—just once or twice, and not during every sequence.

I truly don't believe that we know with any certainty what deer mean with every vocalization they make. Every time a new discovery is made, such as the "grunt, snort, wheeze," somebody immediately comes out with a call to imitate that vocalization. I've been chasing deer with a stickbow for years, and although I've seen a lot of mature bucks interacting, only once have I heard the grunt, snort, wheeze vocalization. A buck made the sound toward a doe that was feeding under the same oak tree as he was, and the only thing I can figure is that he was telling her to leave because he didn't want to share his acorns.

Don't fall victim to every gimmick and gadget that comes out on the market. Get yourself a rattling bag, a grunt call and bleat call, and keep your calling simple. Deer communicate by scent much more than by vocalization, so develop your own scent setup, use the calling and rattling sparingly, and learn what works best in your area by trial and error.

WHEN CALLING AND RATTLING DON'T SEEM TO WORK

Sometimes the best laid traps don't work, and no matter how hard you try, you can't get a buck to respond to your setup. When that happens, it's time to switch gears. We already know that does are the key to finding bucks during the rut. We also know that mature bucks are in a class by themselves, not only because they often remain nocturnal for most of the season (especially if they know they're being hunted), but because they're so extremely cautious to begin with. Remember, they didn't get big by making mistakes.

If you've seen signs of a mature buck in your hunting area but you can't seem to connect with him using conventional tactics, it's time to start using his caution against him. Look for those faint trails we previously talked about that appear downwind of major travel trails and corridors and are likely used by mature bucks who don't want to socialize unless it's with a receptive doe. Also check locations downwind of bedding areas and staging areas where mature does are likely to be found. You may be able to find evidence of one or more mature bucks doing their scent checking here.

These faint trails and scent-checking locations may be anywhere from 50 to 100 yards downwind of major trails, bedding areas, and staging areas, so locating them may require a bit of searching and deduction on your part. You may even have to check in the middle of some of the thickest cover in the area because it's just the place a mature buck not wanting to expose his presence will hide. When searching for these areas, be careful not to leave a lot of your own scent in the area. Just like any other scouting, a one-time in and out session is best. Since these areas are used by mature bucks, I don't recommend using any kind of blind because such a radical change in the environment will be immediately obvious to a big buck. However, a well-placed treestand is just the ticket to elevate you above the action and keep your presence undetected. Just as the buck moves downwind of other deer, you must stay downwind of him. Keeping in mind that you want a good shot within the restrictions of your traditional tackle, place your treestand accordingly within a suitable tree. Because these areas might be very dense with vegetation, even the best stand location may provide only a narrow shooting lane. But since tradi-

Mature bucks often avoid trails used by does and young bucks. Look for faint trails like this one, downwind of heavily used trails to identify where mature bucks are traveling.

tional bowhunters have a sharp instinctive shooting eye and don't have any sight pins or peep sights to contend with, it may be just enough room. Don't, under any circumstances, change the terrain by trimming or adding more shooting lanes. A mature deer is extremely observant to changes in its habitat and, if it feels threatened, may abandon an area completely.

When hunting from treestands in these scent-checking areas, it's critical that the buck not know it's being hunted. Discretion is the key to success. Let the buck come to you rather than trying to draw him in by calling or rattling. If you do call or rattle, he'll most likely stand off at a distance and look for the deer he hears making noise. Carefully apply a small amount of buck urine to try to stop the buck in your shooting lane, but don't overdo it. I use a single scent bomb instead of pouring the scent directly on the ground so that I can remove the scent when I leave the area.

The best time to hunt stands placed near the secondary trails depends upon time of day and time of season. During the pre-rut, big bucks will use these trails to move quietly to and from their bedding and feeding areas, and therefore should be hunted early and late in the day. During the actual rut, they may be on these trails at any given time, so it pays to stay on stand all day. Unlike early and late in the season when you should arrive at your stand before daylight, I frequently wait until it's light enough to see before carefully still-hunting to the stand. This approach increases my opportunity of getting there without being busted by the very buck I'm hunting. Hunting downwind of common bedding areas for doe groups is especially effective at mid-day during the rut. A good time to hunt downwind of staging areas is immediately before dark, when bucks are preoccupied by does that might be in estrous.

During the post-rut, bucks are more concerned with getting their strength back for the winter, so search the downwind side of late-season food sources for faint buck trails. Since bucks want to be left alone, they'll scent check food sources for other deer before coming in to feed.

If nothing else seems to work, try this tactic, which I used several years ago on an evening hunt on Halloween. I knew a mature white-tailed buck was in my hunting area, but I had never seen him. His scent-checking trail was about 100 yards above a crop field frequented by feeding does. The crop field was at the bottom of a wide-open slope, which led up to a fringe of extremely heavy cover bordering another open field. Fortunately, I had located the faint trail he used to check for receptive does down in the field, and had found a tree in the midst of heavy cover, which provided an open shot into one small shooting lane through an opening in the thicket. A single scent bomb I placed on the ground to stop him completed the ambush. As I sat in the tree, I kept my eyes glued to the opening through the thicket because I knew I would get only one shot at this deer. With only a few minutes of shooting light left, I had almost given up when I heard a stick break inside the thick cover. I prepared for the shot, and several minutes later, a large ten-pointer stepped into the opening and stuck his nose into the scent bomb. I buried the shaft from my longbow right behind his shoulder, and the big buck crashed down the slope. The amount of caution this buck displayed was absolutely amazing. From the time I heard the stick snap and managed to find him in the thicket until he stepped into my shooting lane, about ten minutes elapsed. In that period, he only covered about 20 yards, taking one or two steps at a time and then raising his nose and sniffing. Other than the stick breaking, I never heard him make a sound, and he never knew I was there.

Employing patience and stealth in a buck's territory is a fantastic way to kill a mature whitetail, but you also run the risk of spooking him out of the area altogether. Because a buck like this simply will not tolerate intrusion into what he considers his safest areas, I recommend hunting these areas only as a last resort, and never more than once every three or four days.

THE SECOND RUT

The whitetail rut is a wonderful, magical time of the year. It provides the best deer hunting, and if I could only hunt one week of the year, this would be the time. Before we close out this chapter, I want to mention the so-called "second rut," which occurs when does not bred during the first rut come into estrous again in twenty-eight days. I'm hard-pressed to believe that another full-blown rut occurs since by the time these does come into estrous again, the majority of the breeding bucks are worn out and ready to rest. No doubt any buck that has the opportunity to breed an estrous doe will do so, but I don't think that he's going to fight to death to earn that right. He's tired, his health has suffered, and he knows it. He's more concerned with getting his strength and body weight back up to survive the winter. Most likely, any breeding that occurs at this time is done by younger bucks that haven't participated all that heavily in the first rut and are still full of vim and vigor. You can still get a big buck at the end of the season, but you're better off adapting your hunting techniques to late-season food sources instead of trying to hunt as if the rut were in full swing again.

- 8 -

Urban Whitetails and Deer Management

If I told you a serious problem exists in the world of the white-tailed deer, your first thought might be of chronic wasting disease or the importation and exportation of diseased deer between states, or perhaps even "canned hunts" or long-distance hunting over the Internet. Although all of those certainly are legitimate problems, what I'm referring to is the overcrowding of white-tailed deer in urban and suburban America.

Traditional bowhunters are probably closer to the environment and the animals that they hunt than any other sportsmen, a fact reflected by our choice of more "primitive" hunting equipment. Not only are they true stewards of the land and ambassadors of the sport, but bowhunters feel a keen responsibility to the environment and the white-tailed deer that live there. I don't want this chapter to sound like a scientific lecture, which I am not qualified to give anyway, on whitetail habitat or biology, but I believe it's important to have a basic understanding of the explosive whitetail population that is occurring in many locations across the United States and what's being done to solve the dilemma.

Whitetail overpopulation can be attributed largely to the fact that the habitat of the deer is shrinking to the tune of thousands of acres a year. As urban sprawl eats up acre after acre of what was once the white-tailed deer's home, few people realize, and fewer even care, that not only are we ruining irreplaceable natural resources, but we're displacing who knows how many different species of wildlife. Large areas of habitat have been replaced by shopping malls, car dealerships, and residential subdivisions, leaving the deer in particular with no place to go. As a result, deer have learned to adapt to our world, actually living side by side with us in our neighborhoods. What is, at first, a novelty for most urban and suburban dwellers to find the occasional white-tailed deer nibbling grass in their yard soon changes—once the deer start eating prize-winning tulips and making tracks in the flower garden—to a demand that something be done about "all the deer running around and destroying yards and gardens."

Because the white-tailed deer in these less wild areas have fewer natural predators, other than the occasional stray dog, they go about their business without much concern or molestation. They continue to reproduce, which not only increases the population in and around the suburbs, but leads to an increase in damaged lawns and flower and vegetable gardens. More and more, authorities are called in to help rescue a white-tailed deer that has run through the plate-glass storm door or bay window of someone's home and become trapped inside.

In addition to the manicured lawns and small parcels of woods between housing divisions, city parks are also favorite hangouts for "urbanized" whitetails. An excessive deer population damages the ecosystem of the park and results in a petting zoo–like setting when people unknowingly think they're doing the deer a favor by feeding them. This contact with man can cause deer to lose their fear of humans and become dependent on them for food, two problems with obvious consequences.

Most city parks now hold at least a small population of white-tails. In this city park in my hometown, deer are plentiful and a common sight.

Overcrowding of white-tailed deer is not just limited to local areas. Many states have the same problem on a larger scale within their state parks and recreation areas. Wildlife biologists who monitor the ecosystems within these protected areas report the disappearance of certain types of edible plants, the appearance of browse lines along the edges of woods, an increase in car/deer accidents in and around parks, and a visible decline in the general health of the deer population. On suburban farms, white-tailed deer are blamed for severe crop damage. Here in Indiana, the Department of Natural Resources has instituted controlled deer hunts (firearms only, at this time) on many state properties where the deer population has seriously exceeded the carrying capacity of that geographical location. To ensure safety while the hunt is going on, certain areas within the parks become off-limits to vehicular and pedestrian traffic. Such hunts have been occurring for several years, and wildlife biologists report a favorable reduction and control of the number of deer, which allows the flora and fauna to return to its previous state.

Recognizing that a problem exists is the first step in determining the best method for addressing the issue. Over the years, many alternatives have been suggested and attempted, including capture and removal, capture and euthanization, controlled shooting by marksman, birth control, and, imagine this, HUNTING. How the deer population is reduced to controllable numbers is determined by where these problem areas are (their proximity to residential areas and whether they're private or public land) and how much money the responsible government entity has available for deer control.

In 1998, information put together in a single booklet detailed the methods and attempts used by several different states to control their deer population. This informative booklet, called *Case Studies in Controlled Deer Hunting*(c) is available from any state wildlife management agency. Case studies done in New Jersey, New York, Massachusetts, Connecticut, and New Hampshire showed that hunting by itself was an excellent way of maintaining a balanced and healthy deer herd even in areas where deer lived in close proximity to humans. The results of this study have helped many government agencies in their decision to include hunting in their deer-control plans.

Thankfully, most states have recognized hunting as the most viable method of deer reduction and control and have created their own programs for dealing with a very controversial problem. A well-thought-out deer management program has the potential to not only increase a state's revenue through sales of hunting licenses, but it also could further cut costs of the program by allowing the hunters to keep the meat for themselves. State or local governments must pay for processing when culling a deer herd so that precious venison is not wasted.

In areas where the deer population is close to residential areas, bowhunting is an especially effective tool. Bowhunting is less intrusive, safer, and quieter than hunting with firearms.

Although it's not possible to list the locations, laws, and regulations governing every state's Urban Deer Management Program in this book, you can find out all you need to know on the Internet by visiting your particular state's website. While researching this chapter, I learned from a white-tailed deer biologist for the state of Indiana that most people are unaware of the state's Urban Deer Zone program. Quite possibly, other programs could be in place nationwide that would provide traditional bowhunters with new and exciting hunting opportunities as well as the chance to show bowhunting in a positive light.

Hunters have always had to contend with those who would take away our right and privilege to hunt simply because they believe that hunting is cruel and unnecessary. Anti-hunters often are a thorn in the hunter's side, but unfortunately, hunters sometimes put themselves in situations that don't help their cause. For example, practically everyone who has bowhunted long enough has either made a shot on a deer that they wish they could take back or lost a deer they've shot with a bow. Anti-hunters will use reports they've heard of deer running around with arrows sticking out of them as ammunition against us, even though the occurrence of such incidents is frequently beyond our control. But imagine yourself as neutral to hunting and suddenly seeing a deer with an arrow in it stumbling down a road or waking up to find a dead deer with an arrow through its midsection in your backyard? If you're on the fence about hunting rights, such sights might sway you to view bowhunting in a bad light.

That's why if you ever get the opportunity to participate in a deer-management program, it is critical that you practice extreme caution and use good judgment. A few years ago, I read an article written by a bowhunter who had participated in an authorized deer reduction effort at a local golf course. He wrote about still-hunting his way around the outskirts of the golf course and concealing himself from distant joggers. He eventually shot a deer that died in the middle of the golf course, and he wrote of dragging it to a wooded area before he went to get his vehicle.

In another article, a bowhunter wrote about legally hunting so close to a housing addition that he could actually see homes and hear children playing from his treestand. He also claimed a nice deer with his bow and was able to recover it without causing a neighborhood spectacle.

Both of these stories had happy endings because the bowhunters made good shots that ended in the quick death of the deer and a speedy recovery of the animal. When participating in hunts in areas that are more public than our normal hunting grounds, we have a responsibility to maintain the highest standards of ethics and morals so that bowhunting continues as a positive tool for herd control.

GENERAL TIPS AND TACTICS FOR HUNTING URBAN DEER ZONES

If you ever get the opportunity to participate in one of these deer hunts, remember that the main goal of the hunt is to reduce and/or control the size of the white-tailed deer herd within a *specific geographical area*. This means you may have little or no control over where you hunt or what gender of deer you're allowed to take. Find out if other hunters will be in your zone and, if possible, work out a plan with them so you're not all in the same area at the same time. Know the boundaries of the zone, and make sure you understand and adhere to any special instructions that go along with the privilege of participating in such a hunt.

Not all of these hunting opportunities will occur on public land under wildlife management control. Bear in mind that hundreds of acres of suburban farmland located next to many cities, large and small, suffer crop damage from white-tailed deer. Depending on their location, these private farms would normally be off-limits to hunting because of their close proximity to populated areas, but very often these areas are the first places to be designated as Urban Deer Zones, especially if the farmer has contacted wildlife management officials about his crop damage. If you know of a location that may fall into this category, why not check with the farmer or landowner to make them aware of the program and then offer your services in reducing the deer herd in exchange for permission to hunt on their property? It never hurts to stop and ask. Quite often these farmers are looking for good, ethical hunters to come and fill those depredation permits, and most farmers are more likely to allow a bowhunter, rather than a firearms hunter, do the job simply because there's less danger involved. Maybe you'll even be lucky enough to find yourself with an open-ended invitation to return next year.

Regardless of where your deer zone is located, scouting is once again the key to being successful. Once you know what area you have to hunt, get or make a map and go in before your hunt to locate and identify any locations that will tip the odds in your favor. Identify any funnels, fence crossings, or other high percentage areas where you can hang a stand to give yourself an advantage, and then mark these areas on your map for future use.

Unfortunately, deer zones are not based on ideal whitetail hunting habitat. Don't get discouraged if you find yourself in a deer zone that doesn't look like it will be too productive for whitetail hunting. Such situations have happened to me. Before giving up, conduct a thorough search of the area and look for signs of deer, such as a trail or some droppings. When you locate a sign, try to relate it to its surroundings and figure out why the sign is there. Look at the area as a whole and think, if you were a deer, how you would make use of this particular area? Oak trees could provide a feeding area. Pockets of thick cover with trails going in and out could be a bedding area. If you see a trail or two coming through the area, it's likely deer are taking the path of least resistance. If several trails come together, it could be a staging area for deer before they go out to feed. Even in an urban environment, deer are still social creatures and will follow their nature the best they can. It's your job to figure out how they are relating to the piece of ground you're hunting on, and then to hunt that land accordingly.

Here in Indiana, before controlled hunts occur in certain state parks, hunters may go in a few days before the actual hunt to place a stand in their favorite area. Find out from your wildlife management office if this option is available in your state. The quicker you get in the woods to hang your stand, the better off you'll be during the hunt. Good spots will be taken in short order, and you don't want to get stuck with leftovers.

Urban deer hunting is a delicate balance of need and etiquette, and a hunter walks a fine line between doing what is acceptable and what "shocks the conscience." Because you want to avoid any disturbances or confrontations with those who view hunting as wrong, you hope the deer you shoot goes down as quickly as possible and therefore you should only take shots that you know you can make. Once you locate your downed animal, recover it as quickly as possible and don't field dress it until you have it away from the deer zone.

Urban Deer Zones can provide excellent hunting opportunities, especially if you're hard-pressed for places to hunt and don't want to spend a small fortune for a hunting lease or to make a long trip to somewhere else. Just be sure that you are aware of all rules regulating Urban Deer Zones in your area, and don't take anything but high percentage shots. Remember, you are a representative of the traditional bowhunting community.

- 9 -

What Makes a Trophy?

In this chapter, we're going to take a long, hard look at why we as individuals hunt and what actually constitutes a trophy in the eyes of a traditional bowhunter. I'll share my views and philosophies, some of which may not be too popular, and in the process I hope you, the reader, do some soul searching as well. A little honesty with oneself never hurt anybody.

What makes a trophy? To answer that question, we have to decide what motivates us to hunt in the first place. Some philosophers claim that man has a genetic disposition to be a hunter-gatherer and that a predatory instinct drives us to kill our food and feed our families. For some, it's a way of life, a way of continuing an age-old tradition passed from father to son for generations. For others, it's an honorable way of obtaining wholesome food to feed a hungry family.

For me, it's a never-ending road of discovery. I go to the woods to watch and learn about deer, and in the process I often end up learning something about myself as a hunter and a human being. Almost every traditional bowhunter I know feels a *need* to be in the woods, to hunt for game and try to kill that game with the simplest of weapons. I make no apologies for the fact that I kill deer with my bow, and I do not apologize for the fact that I eat meat. Every fall when the sun casts a yellow glow and the breeze starts to cool, I feel a certain calling to grab my longbow and head for the woods.

Even as a young boy before I ever hunted with a bow, I had an overwhelming desire to explore quiet places and stalk blackbirds, rabbits, and squirrels with my secondhand BB gun. Once my family moved to the house where my mother still lives today, I was enraptured with the large broom sage fields surrounding the house. Here, my dad and I would occasionally see a deer or a wild turkey, at a time when either of us hunted anything but small game. Behind our house, a set of fences, about 10 feet apart, separated one field from another. These fences, made of three-strand barbed wire, were completely covered with honeysuckle, which hid anything that traveled between the fences from the outside world. One day, while exploring the field with my BB gun, I happened upon a hole in the fence and entering it, found myself in a whole new world. I followed the trail between the fencerows to a spot where it came abreast of a block of woods at the corner of two county roads.

This block of woods was like heaven for a little boy. Morning glory and Virginia creeper tied every tree in the woods together in a never-ending series of tunnels and arches, each leading to a different part of the woods with a trail of bare earth full of curious tracks. In the middle of the woods, I found a small tarpaper house, abandoned for what could have been ten years or a hundred. Evidence of the previous occupants—an old table and chair, discarded soda bottles, and other odds and ends—was still there. From inside the old home, I could look out and watch the creatures that lived in the woods as they went about their lives. I stalked countless blackbirds, sparrows, and starlings in what I had come to consider my own private hunting ground. When I was there, I was responsible for myself and my surroundings. Even then I deeply appreciated the solitude of the woods and the creatures that lived there, and I knew instinctively that the balance of natural places could easily be upset by carelessness. It was in my boyhood hunting ground that I first learned the importance of woodsmanship, practiced my stalking skills, and recognized the tremendous responsibility of taking the life of an animal, even one as small as a blackbird. That place continued to draw me until the day that a contractor purchased the property, cleaned it up, and turned into a housing addition.

Fortunately for me, my father, a hunter, saw in me the love of the outdoors. He furthered my appreciation for walking in wild places and taught me to appreciate the animals that lived there by taking only what we needed—no more. When I took my first deer, a nice eight-point buck, with the very first shotgun I ever owned, my father was by my side. After the shock of the moment wore off, we walked up to the deer lying dead in the middle of the woods. I still remember my dad's comment as we gazed upon the animal: "Well, what do we do now?"

We struggled through that first field dressing experience, and a couple of years later he took his first deer in those same woods. Later, I would become obsessed with traditional archery, but the foundation for an unbounded love of hunting and an appreciation for all things wild had already been firmly laid, thanks to my dad.

So that's my motivation for hunting, and I strongly suspect that you have a similar love for hunting and wild places, or you wouldn't be standing in the woods each season with that stickbow in your hand.

Unfortunately, the motivation for some hunters is glory and gratification at all costs. What has hurt the world of bowhunting, or any kind of hunting for that matter, is the emphasis placed on antler size. Too many professional hunters will spend what is the equivalent of several years' salary for most of us for the chance to kill an animal with bigger horns or antlers than anyone else so that they get their names in a book and their pictures on the cover of magazines. Many times, they don't even do their own scouting. Someone else will locate the trophy animal, hang the stands, and set up the blinds for them. When you add on the role of sponsors offering money and free equipment in return for endorsements, the true meaning of hunting suffers.

If you look at a large number of books, magazines, videos, and television shows devoted to hunting, for instance, nowhere do you see an eye-catching advertisement for "giant white-tailed does" or "monster fork horns," even though a hunter should be just as proud of bagging a nice doe or fork-horned buck. It's always "monster this" and "mega that." Big antlers sell, period. I suppose hunters are as much to blame for buying into the whole trophy concept as those who are dishing it out. After all, who doesn't dream about drawing a stick and string on a big white-tailed buck with wide, sweeping antlers? The bottom line is you have to ask yourself *why* you want to kill that deer. Do you want to appear a good hunter to your buddies? Do you want him for eye candy on your trophy wall? Do you want a shot at fame and glory, or do you want your name in a book? Or is it because you've done your homework, been a patient hunter, and everything has come together just like you wanted it to? Is the shot a high-percentage one that you've practiced and know you can make?

Big antlers have generated a lot of business for everyone from famous bowhunters to clothing and equipment manufacturers and even seed companies. Many people owe their careers to the whitetail industry and will promote trophy hunting every chance they get, even going so far as to make claims that border on the edge of ridiculous in an attempt to make bowhunters believe that a particular product will guarantee them a chance at a wall hanger. Big antlers have caused people to lie and commit theft, because the glory they were after overshadowed the risks they took to go after it.

My views are not based on jealousy of anyone's success. I'm quite content with and thankful for where I'm at and what I have.

The four-pointer is as much of a trophy as a big buck for a traditional bowhunter.

Deer hunting still holds magic and mystique for me. Despite killing numerous big whitetails with my stickbow, and usually seeing one big enough to make my heart skip a beat every year, I still feel a sense of awe every October when the sun shines *just so,* and the first time a deer strolls past me each season still fills me with excitement, just like it did when I was a boy. For me, hunting is the sights, the smells, the feeling of being in the woods that satisfies an inner desire that I cannot fully explain.

Too often, too many hunters lose track of that magic. They've sold themselves the idea that easier is better, that technology can't be beat, and that they need every little gadget and gizmo that hits the market in order to kill a deer. If anybody had told the Native Americans that, they would've starved.

Most of us who hunt with traditional tackle know it's all about *how we do it,* about setting the highest standards for ourselves and not compromising them for anything. We want to make the playing field level and rely on our own skills as a bowhunter and instinctive shooter instead of using aids to make success come easier. We know hunting is more about the journey and not the destination. Whether it's a carp or an Alaskan brown bear, the pursuit of game with a longbow or recurve is the ultimate hunting challenge. To be successful, you have to do everything right. With no sights to aid you in shooting straight, no laser range finder to tell you the exact yardage, and no release aid to help make a clean release, bowhunting relies on pure skill and concentration. If you don't practice, it shows. You can't put that stickbow aside for nine months out of the year and then expect to hit full draw, much less a target, the next time you pick it up.

I've often been asked why I choose to hunt with traditional bows when the compound bow is so much faster and easier to shoot. I usually just smile, knowing that if they have to ask, they wouldn't understand. The high-tech compound-toting crowd wouldn't understand the hard work and dedication we traditional bowhunters put into our sport. They couldn't possibly believe us when we say that a white-tailed doe taken at 15 feet after a long stalk is a bigger accomplishment than shooting a ten-pointer at 45 yards with a compound. I chuckle to myself when I'm asked, "How do you aim that thing?" and smile at the raised eyebrow when I reply, "I don't." When I recite my "throwing a baseball or football" analogy, I see vague comprehension dawning as they realize that maybe they could learn to do it, too. Instinctive shooting is simple to explain, but proficiency is not easy to attain.

I don't want to leave you with the idea that I believe it's wrong to hunt for trophy bucks, because I don't. Everybody loves the thrill of encountering a mature white-tailed buck with an impressive set of antlers. I enjoy that thrill as much as anyone else, but I recognize it for what it is—the result of being in the right place at the right time. Nothing more, nothing less. A white-tailed buck big enough to have his antler measurements recorded in the Pope and

Young record book does not necessarily make that deer a trophy in *my* book, and sacrificing my own moral character and standards to take that deer is not an option for me. Webster's New World Dictionary defines a trophy, in part, as *anything serving as a reminder, as of a triumph.* By definition, a trophy is a very individual thing, indeed. It can be as intangible as a memory or a photograph or as real as the four-point rack taken from your first bow-killed buck. The most important thing to understand is that the size of the antlers, or even a lack of antlers, has absolutely nothing to do with the true quality of the animal, or of the hunt itself. What is important is what's inside us as traditional bowhunters, how we view bowhunting, and the effort we put forth to make our success. To me, the trophy is the experience of the hunt, the practicing with your bow and not taking shortcuts, and even the passing up a shot at the biggest buck you've ever seen if the conditions aren't perfect. It's about what you do, how you act, and the decisions you make when nobody is beside you in the stand to watch. The trophy is not on any video or in the pages of any book or magazine. It's not even in the woods. The trophy is inside *you.*

- 10 -

Care and Cleaning
in the Field

In my opinion, venison makes the best table fare of any wild game, but if the deer is not handled correctly from the moment it's shot, the taste can be less than desirable. By providing proper care in the field, from the deer's recovery to storing it in a meat cooler, you are taking the first steps to ensure that your deer provides you and your family with the tastiest venison possible.

I used to help out my processor during the busiest part of the season by skinning deer for him. As a result, I've seen my share of deer having to be turned away because the animals weren't taken care of properly after they were killed. What a shame, especially because a few minutes' worth of work and attention to detail could have prevented it.

Proper care begins with good shot placement. If you shoot a deer through its vitals with your traditional bow, the deer will die quickly. If the animal is wounded and runs away, once you catch up with it, dispatch it as soon as possible, not only for humane reasons but also to preserve as much meat as possible. The more pain and panic a deer feels, the more adrenaline that is pumped into its tissues, building up lactic acid, and the tougher and gamier the meat.

Once your animal is recovered, begin the field dressing process as soon as possible. Turn the deer on its back, and either tie the hind legs to a tree to keep them out of the way or have your hunting partner hold them for you. Begin by making a small incision in the center of the abdomen, right below the sternum, with the cutting edge of the knife. Do NOT use the point of the blade, as you may puncture internal organs. Carefully slice through the hair and skin until you can insert two fingers into the abdominal cavity. Then, using your fingers to keep the internal organs pushed out of the way of the knife blade, unzip the abdominal cavity of the deer with the sharp edge of the knife up. The internal organs will probably start spilling out. Just let them go. Remove the sex organs if it is a buck and the milk glands if it's a doe, taking care not to cut the milk glands and flood the meat with milk. Also, make sure that you remove the entire milk gland, including the surrounding fatty tissue. If you're planning on having the deer be mounted, don't cut any farther up on the chest cavity. Your taxidermist will need this part of the hide in one piece for a good mount. If you don't want to have it mounted, continue cutting up through the deer's sternum as far as you can possibly go. Reach into the chest cavity with both hands, being careful to keep track of the knife blade, and cut through the diaphragm the entire circumference of the chest cavity. (The diaphragm is the thin layer of muscle that separates the chest cavity from the abdominal cavity.) Once you've done this, reach as far up as you can, and cut the esophagus and windpipe completely in two. Taking firm hold of these, begin pulling until the internal organs are out on the ground. Now, the only thing that should still be connected to the deer is the large intestine.

Next, make a cut all the way around the anus, as far up as you can, to loosen all the surrounding tissue. Tie a piece of string tightly around the anus, and then reach inside the abdominal cavity to find the large intestine where it travels back above the pelvic bone. Grasp the intestine firmly and pull. You may need to use a bit of force to get it out, depending on how far up you were able to loosen the large intestine and anus. Once all the entrails are removed and the inside of the carcass is cleaned of any excess fat and foreign matter, turn the deer over so that the body cavity can drain. Once all excess blood is drained, wipe down the inside of the body cavity as completely as possible with clean paper towels. If the animal was gut shot and you have access to clean, cold water, hose out the inside of the deer so that all of the stomach or intestine matter is thoroughly washed away. If you don't have adequate water, wipe away as much of the matter as you can with paper towels or clean grass and dry the inside of the body cavity as thoroughly as possible. Some hunters will split the pelvic bone and hams at this time. This helps to cool the meat, which isn't a bad idea if it's going to take some time to drag out the deer and get it to the processor. I also recommend trimming the wide flap of abdominal muscle on both sides of the cut you made down the abdomen. Start at the sternum and, following the ribs, go all the way down to the pelvic area. These flaps of skin are worthless, and removing them will further open up the body cavity and aid in cooling from the inside. The best way to make sure the meat starts cooling quickly is to quarter the animal, if the state you're hunting in allows you to do this before checking it in.

Once you're done field dressing the deer, examine the heart, lungs, and liver for any spots or lesions that could be signs of disease. Also inspect the inside of the body cavity for anything that looks out of the ordinary. If you do observe something unusual, play it safe with a phone call to your local fish and game department to get an expert opinion before taking the deer to be processed. If you keep any internal organs for consumption (there's nothing like fried deer heart with onions on a bun), clean and dry these organs and place them in a separate cheesecloth bag. Be sure you make several deep cuts through the heart to drain as much blood as possible.

When transporting your deer, make every attempt to keep the hide on the animal until it reaches the processor. This will keep the meat clean and deter flies. If the deer has been quartered, wrap the quarters with cheesecloth to protect them from flies and other pests. On particularly warm days, throw a bag of ice or two into the body cavity, if you can, to help the cooling process and if the outside air temperature is going to get above 40 degrees F, try to get the animal inside a cooler as soon as possible.

When you know that the air temperature will not either rise above 40 degrees F or drop below freezing, you can allow the deer to hang in open air for two to three days. But beware—if the temperature drops below freezing at night but not during the day, this constant freezing and thawing process can ruin the meat.

Remember, the best possible way to preserve the flavor and quality of your venison is to field dress the animal quickly and thoroughly clean the body cavity of any blood and excess fat. Transport the deer to the processor as soon as possible, or if you process your own venison, cut up the deer and store it in the freezer as quickly as possible.

If you're going to transport the meat over a long distance, such as from an out-of-state hunting location to your home, bone out as much of the meat as possible (venison starts decaying at the bone) once the animal has been checked in, and pack it in large coolers filled with dry ice. The meat may be frozen by the time you get to the processor, but it will be easier to process in that form.

THE AGING PROCESS

Many different opinions exist on whether or not deer meat should be aged. Proponents say aging allows the naturally occurring enzymes in the meat to begin breaking down the muscle tissue, tenderizing the deer and giving it a more mild and less "gamey" flavor. Some claim that venison should be hung in a cooler for seven to nine days to allow this process to occur. I've spoken with several different processors about this and received several different answers. Some agree with the aging process, but others say that aging is intended for beef cattle and provides no benefits for deer meat. I've even heard an old southern gentleman relate that he used to hang his deer from the head outdoors until the meat started to turn green. He explained that this was how they knew the deer had been aged correctly and was ready to butcher. His story sounds a little questionable to me, especially since he also told me how he they used to hang a duck or goose by the head until the body fell off before he would cook it.

The best advice is to discuss the option of aging the deer with your processor, and find out his or her opinion beforehand.

TAKE CARE OF YOURSELF, TOO

White-tailed deer can carry several diseases, including tuberculosis, brucellosis, epizootic hemorrhagic disease (EHD), and, most recently, chronic wasting disease (CWD). EHD and CWD have similar symptoms, which include abnormal behavior, a weak and emaciated appearance, excessive drooling and urinating, teeth grinding, and drooping head and ears. Although no proof exists that either EHD or CWD can be transferred to humans, I wouldn't want to be the first case. For that reason, I take every possible precaution when field dressing white-tailed deer, or any other wild game for that matter. I always use shoulder-length plastic gloves (like those used by veterinarians) and wear an extra pair of latex gloves over that. That way, I can reach up into the body cavity without getting my sleeves soaked in blood. When I'm completely finished with field dressing, I remove the gloves and put them in a zip-lock baggie for disposal later. Never leave trash behind.

Once you're home, wash your hunting clothes in hot water and a good scent-free laundry detergent to kill any bacteria and para-

A sharp 3- to 4-inch blade is all that's necessary to field dress and quarter a white-tailed deer. Left to right: Emerson folder with 3¹/₄-inch blade and pocket clip; Schrade folder with 4-inch blade and belt sheath; Sharp 4-inch Guthook fixed blade with belt sheath.

sites you may have carried out of the woods. Then wash yourself, taking care to remove any blood under your fingernails.

SOME THOUGHTS ON HUNTING KNIVES

I've field dressed a lot of deer and helped others in the process. One thing that always amazes me is the fact that many hunters, even veterans, carry hunting knives that are big enough to field dress an elephant. Large blades, such as those found on the popular survival and fighting knives, are not necessary and actually make the process of field dressing a deer more difficult and dangerous.

Even the biggest white-tailed buck calls for nothing more than a sharp 3- or 4-inch blade, which easily can be resharpened in the field using the same honing device you use for traditional broadheads. I prefer a high-quality folding knife with a sturdy locking device to make sure the knife will stay open when in use. Fans of the fixed-blade sheath knife should have no trouble finding a version that will fit their needs without making them look like Rambo walking around the woods with a huge knife on their hip.

A regular clip-point or drop-point blade style works best for field dressing and skinning chores. Avoid "Tanto"-style blades and dagger-style boot knives, which are meant for penetration, not for cutting tasks. Multi-tools with a regular knife blade works in a pinch, as long as the blade has a locking mechanism to keep it from closing on your fingers.

Give your hunting knife the same care that you give your hunting broadheads. Make sure you keep the locking mechanism of your folding knives clean and lubricated with a drop of oil. Place a thin layer of petroleum jelly on the edge of the blade to help prevent oxidation and dulling. Sheaths should be kept clean and dry.

TIPS FOR HOME PROCESSING

I know no reason whatsoever that you must have your deer processed by a professional. When I have time or I can't find a processor that has room in his cooler, I cut up my own deer. Because I enlist the help of a couple of interested youngsters, it often makes an ideal project for the entire family.

When processing your own deer, speed is of the essence, especially when the temperature is above 40 degrees F. As soon as you get the deer home, hang it by its hindquarters using a gambrel and take the hide off. (If you're going to have your deer mounted, see the deer-caping tips at the end of the chapter.) Before getting started, gather the following equipment:
- A flat, clean surface at least 4 feet square
- Several rolls of plastic-backed freezer paper
- A sharp butcher knife and a fillet knife, if you have one

- A couple of rolls of freezer tape
- A hacksaw with a coarse blade, or a bone saw

Start by removing one of the deer's forequarters by slicing through the muscle behind the shoulder. Remove the lower leg from the shoulder with a hacksaw, and bone the meat from the lower leg, saving it for stew meat or to grind for burger. You can either bone out the shoulder or cut it in two with the hacksaw to make a pair of shoulder roasts. Do the same with the other shoulder.

Next, saw off the hindquarters at the base of the spine in front of the pelvis, and split the pelvic bone to get two hindquarters. Saw off the lower legs about 6 inches above the knee joints, and bone the meat out for stew meat or burger. Then remove the pelvic bones from the hams, cutting through the thickest part about 6 inches below where you sawed the hindquarters off the carcass. Wrap these as rump roasts.

There are several methods for making steaks from the hams. You can bone the meat out, using a fillet knife to separate the ham from the bone, then cut across the grain to make steaks of any thickness you desire. Or, you can bone the meat out, then separate the muscle groups and make smaller steaks from the individual muscle groups. Or, you can use your butcher knife to cut through the meat to the bone, use the hacksaw to cut through the thigh bone, then finish cutting off the steak with the butcher knife.

Now's the time to remove the backstraps by starting just behind where the shoulders were and cutting down each side of the spine with a fillet knife, if you have one, or your butcher knife, if you don't. The backstrap runs all the way down to the rump, getting smaller as it goes down. Use the blade of the knife to separate the meat from each side of the spine. It will come out in a solid, oval-shaped piece of the finest venison there is to be had. You'll end up with two of them, and you can either cut them in half and freeze them as they are or butterfly them before wrapping. To butterfly the backstraps, simply slice off a 1-inch-thick piece of meat and slice it down the middle from the side, but not quite in two pieces. Fold the cut open, and you have a butterflied backstrap.

The last step is to remove the two tenderloins on the underside of the spine. These are not firmly attached and can be worked loose with your fingers. Cut them loose at each end, and package them separately or, as a special treat, cook them on the grill as you're wrapping meat.

Now, all you're left with are the spine, neck, and head. Bone off any excess meat you want to use for stew meat or burger, and dispose of the rest. Once the meat is wrapped, refrigerate it immediately and clean up your equipment with one part bleach and four parts water to kill any bacteria.

You can either freeze the boned-out meat to be ground later by a deer processor or purchase your own unit to grind the meat into burger. These units vary in capacity and price, but they are a good investment if you decide to cut up your own deer full time. Many books and videos are available that will give you more in-depth information on home deer processing. You can purchase your own home processing kit, which contains all the knives and saws you'll need to do the job quickly and easily.

WRAPPING AND FREEZING SECRETS

The key to preventing freezer burn in any cut of meat is to wrap it very *tightly* so that all air is squeezed out. Make sure the meat is against the plastic side of the freezer paper. Then wrap it again, providing a double layer of protection. When you are done, write the date and the type of cut on the outside of the freezer paper with permanent marker.

If you are fortunate enough to own a vacuum sealer, use it to seal the cuts, then wrap each one in a single layer of freezer paper before marking and freezing. Vacuum packing prevents freezer burn and protects the flavor of your venison. Frozen venison, if packaged properly, can be safely stored in a freezer for up to two years.

Butchering your own deer provides great satisfaction and seems like a natural extension of the entire traditional bowhunting experience. If you involve your family members, they, too, will be wearing smiles when they sit down to a dinner they had a hand in making.

TIPS FOR CAPING A DEER

If you've decided to have your deer mounted, there are several things you will need to do to the deer in the field to get workable material to your taxidermist. You'll need a sharp knife, preferably a skinning knife with a sharp point for detail work, and a sharpening device to keep a keen edge on the blade.

Let's go through the process as though you're going to use the entire cape in the mount. Your taxidermist can cut off whatever he doesn't need. Start by cutting through the hide around the lower legs (your deer should be hanging by them), about 3 inches above the knee joint. Take care not to slice through the large tendon supporting the deer's weight. Then, cut through the hide down the inside of both hams, all the way to where the body cavity opens up.

Using the sharp point of your knife, work the hide loose from each leg until you can get a grip on it. Pull the hide down until it stops. Next, using your fingers, pull the hide away from the deer's rump, all the way up to the tail. Use your knife to carefully cut through the joint that attaches the tail, until you can pull the entire cape down past the rump. Continue to pull, cutting only when necessary, until you reach the top of the sternum.

On the front legs, cut through the hide all the way around, about 4 inches above the knee joint. Slice through the hide inside the front leg all the way to the top of the sternum, at the point where you stopped cutting while field dressing. Using the sharp point of the knife blade, carefully work the hide loose from the sternum around the legs and off the shoulders. At this point, the whole cape should be hanging, gathered around the neck of the deer. Continue to work the hide off as far up the neck as you can. Then use a butcher knife to cut through the neck muscle all the way around and, a hacksaw or bone saw to cut through the neck. Roll the cape up on itself, hair side out, and place it inside a heavy-duty trash bag. Either freeze it or immediately transport it to your taxidermist.

- 11 -

Favorite Venison Recipes

Many folks say they don't like the flavor of venison, claiming it is too strong or too tough. My guess is that those folks have never had a piece of venison that's been cooked correctly. I'd also guess that whoever cooked the meat failed to remove as much of the fat and connective tissue as they should have. The venison itself is not what tastes strong. Rather, the fat, tendons, and connective tissue between the muscles produce that undesirable taste during the cooking process that most people associate with the strong flavor of wild game. For that reason, always use a sharp, thin-bladed knife such as a fillet knife to remove anything that is not red meat from your venison before cooking it.

In addition to proper care and cleaning in the field, moist heat and marinating help to produce a mouth-watering piece of venison, regardless of the cut. What you cook with is also important. Dutch ovens, smokeless indoor grills, and Crock-Pots are wonderful additions to the kitchen range and can add variety to your menus. You can employ a good old charcoal grill or even a bed of hardwood coals to cook an entire meal for you and your family or hunting companions and become a culinary hero in the process.

What follows are some of my favorite venison recipes, ones that I've created or modified over the years to suit my own tastes. Feel free to experiment with them. Any good cook will tell you that's how many top recipes have been created over time. The recipes here are simple, and don't require a lot of fancy ingredients.

MARINADES

A good marinade serves to tenderize the meat and add flavor that will be retained after the cooking process is complete. To create an effective marinade, use a liquid base that contains a lot of acid, such as vinegar, wine, or catsup. My favorite is Italian dressing. It already contains vinegar and spices and tastes great by itself, so it stands on its own as a marinade. However, by adding a few "extra" ingredients, you can make a marinade that's out of this world. If you don't want to make your own, there are plenty of good marinades on the market that can turn a piece of venison into a fantastic feast.

Marinating meat is as easy a task as you can do in the kitchen. Simply place the thawed meat in a flat baking dish, and cover it completely with the marinade of your choice. Then, use a fork to pierce the meat deeply over the entire surface, cover with plastic wrap, and refrigerate for anywhere from four to twenty-four hours, depending on the cut of venison and how much flavor and tenderness you want to impart. For thick pieces of meat such as roasts, use an injector to get the marinade deep into the meat.

BRIAN AND JAMIE'S FAVORITE MARINADE

2 cups Italian dressing
1 cup soy sauce
$1/4$ cup teriyaki sauce
1 tablespoon ground garlic
2 tablespoons barbeque sauce
2 tablespoons Worcestershire sauce

CUTS OF MEAT

There are many different cuts of venison, from roasts and steaks to chops and ground meat. Each has its own particular flavor and tenderness and can be cooked in a number of ways to bring out its flavor. In this section, I've listed recipes according to their cut.

Venison Roasts

Because roasts usually come from areas with a lot of bone, it is easier to cook the meat off the bone than to remove it prior to cooking. Rump roasts and shoulder roasts are the most common cuts on venison, but my processor also makes roasts from the huge necks of rutting bucks that, once cooked, are out of this world. You can also prepare a tender, boneless, rolled roast using a steak and some kitchen string.

Roasts cooked in the oven will dry out quickly if moisture is not maintained. I recommend using a roasting bag, wrapping the roast in bacon, or constantly basting. My preferred method is to cook the roast in a Crock-Pot to maintain moisture and flavor. Here are my favorite recipes. I hope you enjoy them.

CROCK-POT ROAST

1 venison roast, of a size that will fit in your Crock-Pot
3–4 medium potatoes, quartered
2 cups baby carrots
1 package of onion soup mix
2 cups water

Place roast in Crock-Pot and cover with potatoes and carrots. Top with package of dry onion soup mix, then pour 2 cups water over top. Cook on low for 8 hours. Serve with fresh vegetables and crusty bread.

VENISON ROAST ON THE GRILL

1 venison roast (any size)
3–4 slices of hickory smoked bacon, cut into 2-inch long pieces
2 cups of your favorite marinade

Warm up the grill! I like this recipe in the summertime because it gets the cook out of the kitchen. Make several diagonal cuts about $^1/_2$-inch deep all around the roast, and insert the bacon pieces into these cuts. Place roast on the grill over medium heat, basting with the marinade every 10 minutes or so. Flip the roast occasionally until the outside is somewhat crispy and the inside is tender and moist. Cook meat thoroughly. Serve with a crisp salad, corn on the cob, and fresh tomatoes. For a southwestern taste, add hickory or mesquite wood chips to the grill.

PULLED VENISON BARBEQUE

1 venison roast (a backstrap also works well for this recipe)
16–20 ounces of your favorite barbeque sauce
1 cup water

Place roast in an aluminum foil-lined baking pan. Add $^1/_4$ cup of water and cover. Place in 350-degree oven and cook, adding $^1/_4$ cup of water at a time to maintain moisture in pan. Roast is done when it pulls apart easily. Remove meat from bones and discard bones. Stir in barbeque sauce until desired consistency is achieved. Serve on hoagie buns with potato chips and dill pickle spears, or use to top baked potatoes for a hearty meal.

ROLLED VENISON ROAST

1–2 large sirloin steaks
2 cups of your favorite marinade
3 large wooden skewers

Roll steaks tightly from end to end, and pin together using skewers. Place in marinade and refrigerate for 4 to 6 hours. Rolled roast can either be grilled or cooked in Crock-Pot. If you place two steaks together before rolling, you can add red and yellow pepper slices or crushed garlic between the steaks for added flavor.

Backstraps

Backstraps are the tenderest and tastiest parts of a white-tailed deer. In areas where venison is sold in meat markets, backstraps bring the highest price of any cut of venison. The backstrap, which comes from the top of the animal, is found on each side of the spine and runs from behind the shoulders all the way down to the rump. The bigger the deer, the bigger the backstrap. Backstraps are frequently confused with the tenderloins, which are two small strips of very tender meat also found along the spine.

If you butcher your own deer, you can cut up the backstraps any way you want. I recommend freezing them whole, so that you can cook them as a boneless roast, if you want. If later you decide you want them cut, they'll be much easier to cut accurately when they're partially frozen.

Since this strip of meat is tender, flavorful, and boneless to boot, it is frequently cooked without any marinade and very little seasoning. People who complain about the gamey taste of venison would never know they were actually eating it if someone served them, say, a 2-inch thick backstrap filet, which had rested on the grill for a couple of minutes per side before being nestled on a bed of sautéed shiitake mushrooms.

Backstraps are delicious any way you cook them, as long as you don't overcook them. The meat lends itself well to grilling, broiling, and even Southern frying, but it is far too special to be wasted on anything other than careful preparation. What follows are some of my own backstrap recipes, which have been favorites of my family and friends for many years.

SOUTHERN-FRIED BACKSTRAPS AND GRAVY

2–3 pounds of backstrap, sliced or butterflied into $^1/_2$-inch-
   thick steaks
2 cups all-purpose flour
2 tablespoons seasoning salt
$^1/_4$ cup cooking oil
2 cups whole milk
1 tablespoon cornstarch
salt and pepper to taste for gravy

Mix flour and seasoning salt together thoroughly. Heat oil in deep skillet until it smokes. Dredge backstraps through flour mix, and fry for about one minute on each side. Place on paper towel to drain. Set aside.

Add $1^1/_2$ cups of the whole milk to leavings in the skillet and cook over medium-high heat. Add the cornstarch to remaining $^1/_2$ cup milk and mix thoroughly, then stir into liquid in skillet. Stir constantly until mixture is desired thickness, then add salt and pepper to taste.

Serve backstraps with biscuits, fresh green vegetables, and iced tea. Add gravy over meat and/or biscuits.

BREADED "TENDERLOIN" SANDWICHES

2 pounds backstrap, sliced about $^3/_8$-inch thick
$^1/_2$ cup milk
$^1/_2$ cup cooking oil
1 cup all-purpose flour or cornmeal
salt and pepper to taste
kaiser rolls
1 sheet of wax or freezer paper

Start by placing the backstrap slices, one at a time, between a folded piece of wax or freezer paper, then pounding them out with a flat-sided meat hammer or edge of a plate. Soak slices in milk for about a minute, then dredge them through the flour or cornmeal so that all sides are thoroughly coated. Set aside to rest.

Heat oil in deep skillet until oil is hot enough to smoke. Fry breaded "tenderloins" until golden brown on each side, then remove from heat and let drain on paper towels.

Serve on kaiser rolls with all the fixin's, a big plate full of home fries, and fresh lemonade.

TWO-MINUTE GRILLERS

2–3 pounds backstrap fillets, sliced $^1/_4$-inch thick
seasoning salt
2 cups marinade of your choice

This is one of my favorite recipes and is the easiest to make. Marinate your sliced backstraps for 24 hours for maximum flavor. Before you begin grilling, make a big skillet full of fried potatoes and a Caesar salad.

Get the grill fired up to maximum because these medallions will be grilled for only a minute to a minute and a half on each side, depending on how well done you like your meat. Serve with the salad, potatoes, and crusty bread.

BACKSTRAP FILETS WRAPPED IN BACON

> 1 backstrap, cut into 1³/₄-inch to 2-inch-thick fillets
>   (remove membrane or "silverskin")
> enough slices of bacon to wrap around outside of each filet
> seasoning salt to taste

This is a simple yet elegant dish for true venison lovers. Simply wrap a slice of bacon around the circumference of each filet, and secure with a toothpick. Coat both sides of meat liberally with seasoning salt, and allow to "rest" in the refrigerator for 15 or 20 minutes. These filets can be grilled or broiled, depending on your taste. If you decide to grill them, first brown both sides in a skillet with a little cooking oil. Then grill over medium heat until cooked to desired doneness. If broiling, place filets on baking pan and turn occasionally to prevent overcooking. Serve with brown rice and baby carrots for a meal guaranteed to satisfy the hungriest meat lover.

SOUPS AND STEWS

Venison makes a hearty soup or stew, perfect for warming up after a long day on a cold deer stand. Quick, nutritious, and easy to prepare, it also keeps well and can be frozen for future use.

THE WORLD'S BEST VENISON CHILI

> 2 pounds ground venison
> 2 15.5-ounce cans of chili-starter (with or without beans)
> 2 46-ounce cans of tomato juice
> 1 white onion, chopped
> 1 cup elbow macaroni (optional)
> 2 tablespoon of hot sauce or Tabasco sauce (optional)

Brown ground meat and drain thoroughly. In large pot, combine all ingredients except elbow macaroni and bring to boil. Reduce heat, cover and simmer for 30 minutes. Add elbow macaroni and allow to simmer for 10 to 15 more minutes. Serve with oyster crackers. Any leftovers can be reheated or stored in a airtight container in the freezer for future use.

QUICK AND EASY VENISON STEW

2 pounds cubed deer meat (sirloin steaks work best) or ground venison

2 tablespoons cooking oil or bacon fat

4 cups water

2 teaspoons Worcestershire sauce

$1/2$ teaspoon of minced garlic

1 tablespoon of seasoning salt

$1/2$ teaspoon of paprika

6 diced carrots

1 small yellow onion, coarsely chopped

2 cups of diced potatoes

2 beef boullion cubes

Brown venison in skillet with oil or bacon fat. Bring water to boil in a large pan and add all ingredients except onions, carrots, and potatoes (to include leavings from pan). Simmer for about an hour. Add vegetables and cook until vegetables are tender, then season to taste. Serve with good bread and iced tea.

VENISON BURGER

Ground venison is usually restricted to soups, stews, and as an addition to spaghetti sauces simply because deer burger by itself usually doesn't contain enough fat to hold together in a patty or meatloaf form. This can be remedied by adding either ground bacon or beef suet at a ratio of about five parts ground venison to one part ground bacon or beef suet. You can do this yourself, or ask your deer processor to add suet or bacon to your ground venison when it's processed.

VENISON RANCH BURGERS

2–3 pounds of ground venison (with suet or ground bacon added)
2 packages of dry Ranch dressing mix
2 green onions, finely chopped

For those of you who crave something new in the world of burgers, this is it. Simply mix all ingredients thoroughly in a large bowl, cover with a towel, and allow to stand in the refrigerator for an hour. Make patties as usual and cook on the grill or in the broiler. Serve on sesame seed buns with shoestring potatoes and all the fixin's.

A-1 VENISON MEATLOAF

2 pounds of ground venison
2 cups of soft bread crumbs
$^1/_2$ cup beef broth
$^1/_2$ cup chopped onion
2 eggs, slightly beaten
$^1/_4$ teaspoon dried oregano
$^1/_4$ teaspoon pepper
$^1/_4$ teaspoon salt
1 small can of tomato paste

Heat oven to 325 degrees. Grease a 9-inch by 5-inch pan with butter or Crisco. Mix all ingredients except tomato paste in a large bowl and shape into a loaf in pan. Bake until browned, about an hour and a half, then add tomato paste to top of meatloaf. Bake for an additional 5 minutes, then remove from oven and serve. Goes great with macaroni and cheese and a pasta salad.

These are just a few of the many recipes I enjoy, and all of them are adaptations on time-proven recipes normally used for beef. Remember, the keys to cooking a good piece of venison are to marinade whenever possible and don't overcook it. Overcooking results in a radical loss of moisture, which ends up as a tough piece of meat.

Several wild-game recipe books on the market have many more recipes for venison. Some are elegant and time-consuming to prepare, while others are quick and easy. Every year, I talk to a lot of hunters who just don't enjoy eating their venison, and usually it's because they're trying to cook it like they would a piece of beef. With careful preparation on your part, you'll soon learn that venison is not only healthier than any beef on the market, but it can be just as delicious.

- 12 -

Introducing Kids to Traditional Bowhunting

Remember when you were a kid? Did you have one of those little white fiberglass bows with suction-cup arrows? I did, and it got me in a bit of trouble when I began experimenting with different arrow shaft materials at the early age of five. Even then I had a love of stalking things with the bow and a desire to watch the arrow in flight.

But, bowhunting for deer was light-years in my future, mostly because the only one bowhunting back then was the likes of Fred Bear, and few deer lived in the area where I grew up. As a matter of fact, just seeing a white-tailed deer in my community was an exciting event and the talk of the town for quite some time.

When I did begin hunting, it was for small game such as squirrels and rabbits. Under the watchful eye of my father, I slowly worked my way up through the various gauges of shotguns until I could handle his old twelve gauge comfortably. Because we always hunted on Saturday mornings, I spent Friday nights in fitful sleep, waking up every hour or two to make sure I hadn't overslept. Little did I know then that this youthful enthusiasm was only the beginning of my love affair with hunting. I would spend many more nights in exactly the same fashion, waking up to glance occasionally at my stickbow, dutifully standing in the corner, waiting for me to get up and go hunting.

Many years passed between my first small-game hunting and chasing whitetails with the traditional bow, but my desire to hunt never grew dim. Every fall it would be fanned into a full flame, driving me to the woods. I can't say exactly what it was that made hunting such a passion for me. I know that it was something I enjoyed sharing with my dad, who taught me woodsmanship, ethics, and safety, but I suspect there was more to it than either he or I could understand. Whatever it was, it didn't take much encouragement to bring out my passion for hunting.

The world today is a different place than when I was young. The Internet and video games compete for a child's important time outdoors. Any stalking or target shooting usually takes place on a television or computer screen via a joystick controller.

I think it's time for us to reintroduce the traditional bowhunting heritage to our children, although a word of warning is necessary: Don't push too hard lest we push them away completely. Children are constantly bombarded by information from all different types of media. They are presented with a variety of opinions on subjects as diverse as tobacco use to (dare I say it?) animal rights. Cartoons and the personification of animals have led children to view animals in a different light than what God intended. Yes, Bambi's mother *was* shot by a hunter in the Disney classic. In a hunting household, the children may have asked what kind of gun or bow the hunter used. In a non-hunting household, the parents often have to explain what happened to Bambi's mother because the children may have no idea what hunting is. In an anti-hunting household, the parents would have sat the children down before the movie ever started and pointed out that hunting is wrong and that Bambis all over the United States lose their mothers every fall when inhumane deer hunters take to the woods. Some kids are given good information about hunting, some are given the wrong information, and some are given no information at all. It's up to us to make sure they learn the difference between what's right and acceptable about hunting and what's illogical and incorrect.

I think it's best to ease kids into the whole concept of bowhunting. Start them out target shooting with a good bow at an early age. Both of my daughters had bows by the time they were five: Rachel had a fiberglass laminated longbow, and Claire had a hickory-backed cherry selfbow. They both had matching arrows and enjoyed shooting their bows. They learned to enjoy the flight of the arrow and the challenge of instinctive shooting, and under my watchful eye, they taught themselves as much as I taught them. With a little coaching and guiding of their instincts, they took over like they knew what they were doing. They never wanted compound bows, just bows like Daddy's, and the thought of getting them compound bows never occurred to me because I don't want them growing up thinking everything in life can be done with gadgets. I want them to know they can rely on what's inside them.

How young you start a child in bowhunting is up to you. Youth bows and arrows that will fit even the smallest future traditional bowhunter are available from suppliers such as Kustom King Archery and 3 Rivers Archery Supply. I recommend installing the No-Glov on the bowstrings of really little shooters. These rubber pieces slip over the bowstring to provide a positive nocking point and to protect little fingers from the bite of the bowstring. They also allow the string to roll off the fingers easily and cleanly, making for a better release. Make sure a child is shooting bows that are not too heavy or too big, and upgrade the size and draw weight of their bows as they get bigger and stronger. Also provide correctly spined arrows to shoot from their bows.

Teach children the basics of instinctive shooting, such as how to nock an arrow correctly and how to hold the bow. Show them how to string and unstring a bow properly. Constantly drive home the

My daughters Claire (left) and Rachel love to shoot their traditional bows. Claire has a hickory-backed cherry Selfbow, and Rachel has a fiberglass laminated Bubinga longbow. Both shoot $^1/_4$-inch cedar shafts with 4-inch shield-cut feathers.

fact that a bow is not a toy and is never, ever to be pointed at a person. Finally, get out and shoot with them. Let them see how much you enjoy hunting, and share that joy with them. Never force them to shoot, but always encourage them. If they overdo it, they could become too frustrated.

When you take a deer, bring it home, if possible, so your children can see where all that meat comes from. My kids actually get upset with me if I don't bring a deer home to show them before it goes to the processor. Let them touch the animal and get used to the idea that this was once a living, breathing creature. And above all, ALWAYS show respect for the animal. Don't allow any clowning around with the carcass, or any silly pictures to be taken. If you show respect for the animal, your children will respect it as well and understand the seriousness of taking an animal's life. Recount the shot with them, and show them the entry and exit holes, explaining how the broadhead did its job. Let them see the arrow that you used to take the deer, so that they can understand the lethality of the bow and arrow.

How do you know when your child is ready to hunt? It's a highly individual decision, but most states have age limits that determine the age that a child may hunt. Most states also have weight limits for archery equipment, and this will dictate a certain size and strength requirement. It is unethical to allow a child to hunt with equipment that will not do the job, or with skills that are not up to the task. My advice is that your child should be capable of shooting at least 35 pounds of draw weight at their draw length before attempting to hunt deer. They should also be capable of shooting tight, accurate groups out to a range of about 15 yards with their broadhead hunting arrows.

I recommend beginning with small game such as rabbits and squirrels so that the child becomes used to the idea of shooting a live animal. You might even have the child try a small-gauge shotgun or small-caliber rimfire rifle, just to see how he or she reacts to

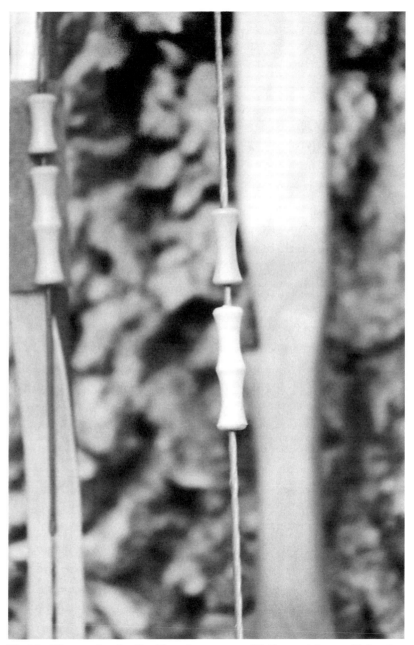

The No-Glov, made of soft rubber, does away with the need for small shooting gloves or tabs. Both of my daughters shoot well with them.

taking game. Monitor the process closely, and watch for signs of disinterest or aversion. Never force the child to shoot an animal. Instead, be encouraging and supportive, letting him or her gain acceptance at his or her own pace. Take children scouting with you, and let them explore the woods and natural world for themselves. Answer any questions as best you can, and if you don't know the answer, tell them that instead of making something up. Then once you get home, log onto the Internet and find the answer together.

No matter how hard we try, our efforts are not always rewarded as we like. Children may have no interest in hunting, but they may love shooting 3-D targets with their bow. Maybe they have no interest in traditional archery at all. Or, perhaps they're just late bloomers who will develop an interest later on. The key is to always provide them with good equipment and always have the time to help and show them the right way to do things. Never leave children on their own to shoot.

When a child's skills and interest have developed to the point where he or she wants to hunt whitetails, you must forego your own hunting when taking them. Start out by placing a two-man ladder stand over an area with a high concentration of does and young deer, so that the child gets exposed to quite a few animals. In fact, don't even take a bow the first time or two out. Let the child get used to being around deer and to learn how to move slowly and quietly in the deer's presence.

When the time finally comes and you think your child is ready to hunt whitetails with a traditional bow, be there with him or her every step of the way. Help her during the shot selection process. Calm his nerves, and never let him take a shot outside his effective range or if he's too nervous and shaky. Celebrate the misses and successes equally, making sure that she understands that even getting a shot is an accomplishment in itself. In short, teach your child to be an ethical, responsible sportsman. The ability to mold a new traditional bowhunter is in your hands. Make sure you do it right.

Appendix

Bowhunting Suppliers

Traditional bowhunting is a simple sport, but it requires special equipment that often can't be bought at your local sporting goods store. Thankfully, more and more catalogs are carrying traditional archery supplies, and a slew of suppliers provide bowhunters with excellent choices and service.

What follows is a short list of traditional bowyers, some of whom offer traditional archery supplies in addition to custom bows, and traditional archery suppliers, some of whom carry quality traditional bows as well as archery supplies. Most of these companies produce catalogs of the items they carry.

Black Widow Custom Bows
1201 Eaglecrest
P.O. Box 2100
Nixa, MO 65714
(417) 725-3113
www.blackwidowbows.com

Black Widow sells custom recurves and longbows, as well as bows by Martin Archery and other manufacturers. It also offers traditional supplies and accessories.

3 Rivers Archery

P.O. Box 517

Ashley, IN 46705

(260) 587-9501

www.3riversarchery.com

3 Rivers is the world's largest traditional archery supplier. The list of bows, equipment, and accessories it carries is far too large to mention here. Suffice it to say that they have *anything* you could possibly need that's related to traditional archery.

Kustom King Traditional Archery

5435 75th Avenue

Schererville, IN 46375

(877) 566-4629 toll-free or (219) 322-0790

www.kustomkingarchery.com

Kustom King is known the world over for its beautiful hand-crafted wood arrows. It also has a complete line of traditional archery gear, all of which is mail order only. No showroom.

Cabelas

One Cabelas Drive

Sidney, NE 69160

(800) 237-4444 toll-free

www.cabelas.com

Cabelas offers a complete line of hunting and fishing gear. It also carries traditional archery tackle as well as a complete line of treestands, game calls, scents, and deer lures.

Fox Archery
Ron King
701 West Highway 82
Wallowa, OR 97885
(541) 886-9110
www.foxarchery.com

Ron King at Fox Archery makes the best longbow I've ever shot. He also creates custom recurves and offers both styles in a takedown configuration. Custom bow orders only.

Alaska Bowhunting Supply
14000 Goldenview Drive
Anchorage, AK 99516
(907) 345-4256
www.alaskabowhuntingsupply.com

Ed Schlief at ABS is the creator of the fabulous Grizzlystik arrow shaft, which is my favorite. Ed also offers such items as seal-skin shelf rest material, handmade knives, and Cordovan leather shooting gloves and tabs.

Wapiti Recurves and Longbows

J. K. Chastain, Master Bowyer
490 S. Queen Street
Lakewood, CO 80226
(303) 989-1120
www.worldclassbows.com

Kieth Chastain has been making bows for more than 35 years, and his takedown and one-piece recurves and longbows have one of the best warranties in the business. He also offers Port Orford cedar shafts by Rose City Archery.

Timberhawk Bows, Inc.

Scott Mitchell
7895 State Road 446
Bloomington, IN 47401
(812) 837-9340
www.kiva.net/~thawk

Scott Mitchell makes beautiful longbows and recurves. His longbows especially captured my eye because of the way he puts quite a bit of reflex/deflex into the limbs and still maintains the classic "D" shape of the longbow. Quality and craftsmanship are present in each bow he makes.

Robertson Stykbow
P.O. Box 7
989 Stykbow Lane
Forestgrove, MT 59441
(406) 538-2813
www.robertsonstykbow.com

Dick Robertson and his son Yote produce high-quality, hand-crafted bows that are one of a kind. I highly recommend a visit to their website. But be forewarned, you'll probably end up ordering a bow.

Index

lock-on (fixed-position),
    82–84
placement of, 86–88
practicing from, 39
safety issues and systems, 79,
    84–86
strategies, 89–90
trophies, 149–152
two-minute grillers, 171

U
U.S. Geological Service, 52, 101
urban areas, deer management,
    138–145
urine scents, dominant buck
    and doe-in-heat, 120–121

V
venison ranch burgers, 174
venison roast on the grill, 167
vision, 61, 65, 67
vital zones, making a quick kill
    and the, 34–37

W
Wapiti Recurves and Long-
    bows, 6, 186
whitetails
    anatomy of, 34–37
    antlers, 31–32
    breeding, 29–31
    habitat of, 32–33, 45–47
    physical description of, 29
    range of, 27–28
Wildlife Research Center, 125
wind, using, 64–65, 73–74
world's best venison chili, the,
    172–173